DECEIVING AMERICA

Progressive Deceit and the Danger
to American Freedoms

THOMAS MOORE

DEFIANCE PRESS
& PUBLISHING

DEFIANCE PRESS
& PUBLISHING

ISBN-13: 978-1-963102-33-8 (Paperback)
ISBN-13: 978-1-963102-32-1 (eBook)

Published by Defiance Press & Publishing, LLC

Bulk orders of this book may be obtained by contacting Defiance Press & Publishing, LLC. www.defiancepress.com.

Public Relations Dept. – Defiance Press & Publishing, LLC
281-581-9300
pr@defiancepress.com

Defiance Press & Publishing, LLC
281-581-9300
info@defiancepress.com

Chapter 4 is dedicated to those who fought in the WWII Pacific Theater.

Table of Contents

Note to the reader: Due to formatting, some footnotes are at the bottom of the pages throughout the text, while others had to be placed at the end of the respective chapter.

Preface

As the Xennial, or Oregon Trail, generation was growing up through the 1980s and 1990s, we were told we had opportunity in America. It was always known that many people were less fortunate than we were, to appreciate what we had and to be humble. Three decades ago it felt like Americans had an unspoken bond and were supportive of one another. After the September 11, 2001, terrorist attacks, we were drawn even closer.

A generation later, as the young people who watched the atrocities of 9/11 on TV inch toward middle age, a lot has changed. High-speed internet, smartphones and social media now allow us to access information with the tap of a finger and headlines are often the only part of the news that many people read. Information gets out to millions of people within seconds and with it, unfortunately, comes propaganda and misinformation. Like never before, the media, politicians, corporations, celebrities and even average folks push propaganda-based narratives so regularly and intensely that it has become hard to know what is factual, fictional, and which important stories or statistics are not being reported.

Division has become rampant. The American people have been categorized and divided by our race, wealth, personal medical decisions, or even by whether or not we support local law enforcement! This has been enabled by much of the media, social media and education systems throughout the country. The narratives of critical race theory, smooth and fair elections being voter suppression, police being the bad guys (or gals), or that the Constitution of the United States doesn't work for its people are all false narratives. These are some of the many lies we are being told every day, intended to divide and weaken us as a whole. These are the lies the radical (or Progressive) left is telling us. The far left doesn't make up a large portion of our population, but they have a strong, loud base and control today's Democratic Party.

The following chapters prove these narratives are false, dangerous and how those the Progressives claim to help are the ones being hurt the most. They provide a brief history of many important and relevant events in American History that prove the effectiveness of the Bill of Rights and the Supreme Court as well as the significance and sacrifice so many have made fighting for our personal liberties!

PART ONE

Chapter One

Over an eleven-year period, Professor Pesta, an English professor at the University of Wisconsin-Oshkosh, gave his students quizzes at the beginning of the school year to test their knowledge of basic facts on Western culture. The most surprising finding was how many students believed slavery began in and was exclusive to the United States.

How could this be, you ask? Is it what our children are being taught at school? At home? On the internet? Are people just unaware? Is our youth being indoctrinated?

THE FACTS

It has been difficult for historians to pinpoint precisely when slavery began, as its origins can be traced back before the written word. The earliest concrete evidence of its existence comes from the Code of Hammurabi out of Mesopotamia.

The Code of Hammurabi was one of the earliest and most complete written legal codes. It was proclaimed by the Babylonian King Hammurabi, who reigned from 1792 to 1750 BC. This code, or ancient law, outlines the three classes of Babylonian society: the propertied class, freedmen and slaves. Slavery was described as a common practice that had been part of society for thousands of years at the time it was written, giving strong evidence that it was part of the culture as far back as at least 7,000 BC.

Slavery continued as a part of society through ancient times. Many Israelites were enslaved by the pharaohs in Egypt in the 1000s BC and this practice continued through Ancient Roman and Greek societies, where it was accepted and profited from. Those who were captured in war were often kept by the conquering power as slaves. Piracy was a large and consistent factor in the slave trade as well.

The ancient Greek philosopher Aristotle (384 BC to 322 BC) had a very disturbing view on slavery, believing human beings came in two types: slaves and non-slaves. Here are two quotes from Aristotle: 1) "Some should rule and others be ruled is a thing not only necessary, but expedient; from the hour of their birth, some are marked out for subjection, others for rule" 2) "And indeed the use made of slaves and of tame animals is not very different; for both of their bodies minister to the needs of life."

Many of us have heard Progressives such as Bernie Sanders refer to the Scandinavian countries of Norway, Sweden and Denmark when talking about a model for their vision of the United States. First, this doesn't make sense—those countries are actually more capitalistic than the US! We will talk more about that later. Second, it needs to be noted that no country has a "pure" history. Between the years 800 AD and 1200 AD, the Vikings resided in the region known as Scandinavia and were actively involved in the slave trade. Does that mean we should blame the Swedish for the actions of their ancestors…? Hah! No, of course not—we should teach history as it happened and learn from it!

It is taught that slavery is racial in nature—something that White people did to Black people. This is true in terms of ownership of slaves in the United States, but it hasn't always been the case. In the transatlantic slave trade, Africans were generally sold to Europeans by other Africans, usually in exchange for guns, gunpowder, cloth, beads, alcohol, or household goods. Many of those sold were already enslaved, often due to capture from other tribes.

From the 1500s to the 1700s, pirates along the coast of North Africa raided ships in the Mediterranean Sea, Atlantic Ocean, and seaside villages in Italy, Spain, and France, capturing men, women and children. England, France and Spain each lost thousands of ships, and long stretches of the Spanish and Italian coasts were largely abandoned as a result. An estimate by author and history professor Robert Davis calculated that between 1 and 1.25 million Europeans were captured and forced to work in North Africa during this period, and the destruction and depopulation of some areas probably exceeded the damage that Europeans would later inflict on Africa's interior. Contrary to the narrative of the far left, there was a time and place where lighter-skinned Europeans were enslaved by darker-skinned Africans.

★ ★ ★

The transatlantic slave trade that most readers are aware of was every bit as bad as it is taught, probably worse. It began in 1526 when Spanish explorers brought the first African slaves to what would later become the United States. This is contrary to the narrative of *The 1619 Project*, as the Spanish bringing Black slaves across the Atlantic must not fit the agenda of its writers. From 1526 to the early 1800s, it is estimated that 12 to 15 million Africans were shipped across the Atlantic and that another two to six million did not survive the terrible voyage.

The British, Portuguese, Dutch, Spanish and French were all major participants in the transatlantic slave trade, with the British responsible for taking roughly 40 percent of the total slaves to the Americas. Almost half of the Africans taken across the Atlantic were sent to the Caribbean Islands of Jamaica, Barbados or Saint-Domingue (known today as Haiti). About 40 percent were sent to Brazil, which was the shortest voyage from West Africa, taking approximately a month.

During the entirety of the colonial slave trade, only about five percent of all slaves were sent to what is now the United States.

Many victims of the transatlantic slave trade were already enslaved in Africa, often as far as 300 miles from the coast. The captives were chained by the ankles and marched 300 miles to the Atlantic Ocean to be sold. Historians estimate 10 to 15 percent died before they made it to the coast.

The Atlantic crossing, or Middle Passage, was the dreadful time when slaves were shipped from the west coast of Africa to the Americas to be sold. During this passage, hundreds of Africans were chained and crammed into ships with ceilings so low, they often were not able to sit upright. The average slave only had about four square feet of space. There were very high mortality rates on these ships for both slaves and crews, mostly due to yellow fever and malaria.

Chapter Two

As the American colonies were expanding in the late 1700s, a great rift was developing between the colonists and Great Britain. The British Parliament began to pass taxes the colonists were required to pay, such as the Townshend Acts. Passed in 1767, the Townshend Acts required the colonists to pay taxes on imported goods such as tea, lead, paint, paper and glass. They were repealed three years later in 1770 except for the tax on tea. Most readers probably remember learning about the Boston Tea Party that occurred in December of 1773, where the colonists dumped 342 crates of tea, imported from the British East India Company, into the Boston Harbor.

In response, the British Parliament established the Coercive (or Intolerable) Acts in March 1774. The Intolerable Acts closed the port of Boston until the damages from the Tea Party were paid and introduced the Quartering Act of 1774 that empowered Britain to find quarters for their soldiers in the colonies, generally in barracks, barns or other buildings.

As tensions continued to build between the British government and the American colonies, delegates from twelve of the thirteen colonies met in Philadelphia in September 1774 to discuss a plan of action. This became known as the First Continental Congress. The delegates were chosen by the people and many of their names, such as George Washington of Virginia or John Adams of Massachusetts, are famous in American History. At this momentous meeting, it was decided the colonies would stay loyal to Britain but stop importing British goods.

★ ★ ★

The Revolutionary War officially began on April 19, 1775, when gunfire erupted between minutemen from the American colonies and British soldiers in the battles of Lexington and Concord. The following year, the Second Continental Congress met and voted to approve the Declaration of Independence on July 2, 1776, declaring the colonies as free and independent states. The final draft was approved on July 4, marking Independence Day for the United States of America.

> We hold these truths to be self-evident, that all men are created equal, that they are endowed by their Creator with certain unalienable Rights, that among these are Life, Liberty and the pursuit of Happiness. That to secure these rights, Governments are instituted among Men, deriving their just powers from the consent of the governed […]

The opening of the Declaration of Independence, listed above, and the US Constitution written about a decade later are the framework that has made the United States one of the greatest countries on earth. There is no country with a pure history, and there is no doubt that there have been many injustices throughout American history. Our Constitution, however, is not broken. In fact, it is logical and represents freedom! The Constitution was designed to provide a limited government by developing three branches and allowing them to have checks and balances over one another. It also provides for a balance of power between the federal and state governments, the ability to make changes by adding amendments or passing legislation without changing its form or founding principles, and of course, the people having their *say* with the right to vote.

FOUNDING FATHERS AND SLAVERY

Some of our Founding Fathers were slave owners and some were not. This new government was created in the middle of the American Revolution, with the primary goal to gain our freedom from Britain. Many of our Founding Fathers acknowledged that slavery existed in contrast to the core values of liberty and freedom—the pillars of the new American government.

Benjamin Franklin, a slave owner earlier in his life, spent much time in his later years speaking out against slavery. In 1789, he published several essays supporting the abolition of slavery, and the following year he sent a petition to Congress asking for its abolition. The petition signed in February 1790 asked Congress to "devise means for removing the inconsistency from the Character of the American People" and to "promote mercy and justice toward this distressed Race." Franklin also published Quaker pamphlets against slavery in his younger years.

Benjamin Franklin

The topic of our Founding Fathers and slavery is controversial. Slavery was undoubtedly inherited, and the Fathers created the foundation for everyone in the United States to enjoy the freedoms we have today, but many of them were not yet willing to give up their personal way of life—which involved having slaves. Later generations would make great sacrifices to abolish slavery as the abolitionist movement picked up in the early 1800s.

LA AMISTAD

In 1839, thirty-one years after the transatlantic slave trade was abolished in the United States, a Spanish ship called *La Amistad* was found off the coast of Long Island. On the ship were a group of Africans who had been captured from what is present-day Sierra Leone and were being taken as slaves to Cuba to work for two Spanish plantation owners. During the voyage, the slaves had revolted at sea and taken control of the ship, killing two of their captors.

The Africans were kept in jail in New Haven, Connecticut, while the courts decided their legal status. The Spanish plantation owners Pedro Montes and Jose Ruiz, the Spanish government and Democratic President Martin Van Buren all wanted to send the Africans to Cuba, where they would be slaves.

The US District and Circuit Courts ruled, however, that the Africans had been illegally captured and were to be returned to Africa. The case was appealed to the Supreme Court, where former President and current member of the House of Representatives John Quincy Adams defended the Africans. The following is a quote from John Q. Adams to the Supreme Court:

> "The moment you come to the Declaration of Independence, that every man has a right to life and liberty, an inalienable right, the case is decided. I ask nothing more in behalf of these unfortunate men, than this Declaration."

In March 1841, the Supreme Court ruled 7-1 to uphold the lower courts' decisions in favor of the Africans. After the decision, abolitionists raised funds for the Africans to return to their homeland across the Atlantic. From the Amistad Case in 1841 to recent rulings in 2021 and 2022, our Supreme Court has most often worked to uphold the Constitution.

Contrary to what many people today want you to believe, many constitutionalists and conservative-leaning men such as Benjamin Franklin and John Quincy Adams fought for fairness and individual liberties for all!

John Quincy Adams

John Quincy Adams (the sixth president) and his father John Adams (the second president) were the only two of our early presidents to never own any slaves. John Q. Adams believed slavery was immoral.

Possibly the worst Supreme Court decision in American history was *Dred Scott v. John F. A. Sandford*. Dred Scott was the slave of an army surgeon who sued for his freedom in 1846. A decade later, his case reached the Supreme Court and a ruling was made in 1857. The Court ruled 7-2 that Scott, as a Black man, was excluded from US citizenship and therefore could not bring suit. This decision was majorly wrong, given the Constitution has no mention of race, ethnicity or skin color.

Who were the justices who ruled on the case? The seven justices who concurred that Black people were not citizens—Taney, Wayne, Catron, Daniel, Nelson, Grier and Campbell—were all Democrats. Three of these men were nominated by Andrew Jackson, who owned two hundred slaves and signed the Indian Removal Act of 1830, leading to the Trail of Tears. The two justices who dissented, McLean and Curtis, were both Republicans at the time of the ruling.

Does this mean we should blame today's Democrats for this ruling? No, of course not—nor should we blame Republicans or anyone else who is alive today. People from both sides of the political spectrum try to mend American history to fit their narrative when we should be learning history as it actually happened. Political parties change over time—just look at how much both major political parties in America have changed in the last decade. The Republican Party has become more isolationist, populist and vocal against elites and big government rather than the more compliant, soft-spoken "silent majority" of decades past. The Democratic Party has transformed from one of liberal ideals that supported fiscal safety nets into a radical left ideology that supports revolutionary reform and a huge central government.

We have to look at the facts and make a decision as to what is best for our families, our communities and our country moving forward. And the facts show that supporting today's Democratic Party is not what is best...

Chapter Three

Sometime in the fall of 1849, Harriet Tubman decided to escape from slavery for good. Traveling only at night, she followed the North Star to freedom, eventually arriving in Philadelphia. Harriett Tubman was born a slave named Araminta Ross (nicknamed Minty) on a large plantation in eastern Maryland around the year 1821. She hated slavery and wanted to help her enslaved family and as many others as she could.

In Philadelphia, Tubman became familiar with the Underground Railroad and got to know many of the "conductors." She became a conductor herself, making a total of nineteen journeys into the South between 1850 and 1860 to lead slaves north to freedom. After the Fugitive Slave Act was passed in 1850, she would often have to lead them all the way to Canada. Over the years she rescued over seventy slaves, including many of her own family and never failed on a single rescue.

When the Civil War broke out in 1861, Tubman fought slavery in different ways by becoming a nurse and later a spy for the Union Army. When she wasn't on the battlefield nursing wounded Union soldiers, she was often making breads, pies, and even her own medicines for them. After 1863, Tubman became the head of an espionage and scout network for the Union Army, going behind enemy lines to bring back information about the positions of Confederate armies and gun batteries. Tubman also helped form Black Union regiments.

After the Civil War, Tubman returned to the property she had previously bought in 1859 in Auburn, New York. She continued to speak for the rights of Black people and also for women's suffrage. Harriet Tubman never met Abraham Lincoln and did not speak highly of him until after the Civil War, when her views changed after a former slave named Sojourner Truth told her of Lincoln's kindness. Sojourner Truth had met Lincoln in 1864 to thank him for signing the Emancipation Proclamation.

Tubman did know Lincoln's Secretary of State William Seward and his wife, Francis. Tubman and Seward had shared a common goal of abolitionism, and Seward's home in Auburn, New York, was part of the Underground Railroad. It was actually Seward who sold Tubman her property in Auburn. After the Civil War, Seward immediately advocated that Tubman receive a government pension for her service as a nurse and a scout in the US Army.

Harriet Tubman (1823 – 1913)
nurse, spy and scout

Harriet Tubman

William Seward

    William Seward (above) was a member of the Whig and later Republican parties who, in addition to being secretary of state under Lincoln, served as governor of New York from 1839 to 1842 and as a United States senator from 1849 to 1861. After defeating Seward in the Republican Party primary and winning the presidency, Lincoln appointed him as secretary of state, where he remained until 1869.

★ ★ ★

In May of 1860, Abraham Lincoln upset William Seward for the presidential nomination of the Republican Party and went on to win the general election that November. Lincoln was opposed to slavery on moral grounds, opposed to its expansion and very much wanted to preserve the Union. On April 12, 1861, just a month after Lincoln's inauguration as the sixteenth president, the Civil War began.

★ ★ ★

In November 1863, President Lincoln traveled by train to Gettysburg, Pennsylvania, to honor those who lost their lives in the deadliest battle in the American Civil War. The evening before and the morning of November 19, 1863, Lincoln worked on his speech that would become known as the Gettysburg Address. Finally, when it was the president's turn to speak on that November day, he stood up and delivered his two-minute 270-word classic.

> "Fourscore and seven years ago our fathers brought forth on this continent, a new nation, conceived in Liberty and dedicated to the proposition that all men are created equal. Now we are engaged in a great civil war, testing whether that nation, or any nation so conceived, and so dedicated can long endure. We are met on a great battle-field of that war. We have come to dedicate a portion of that field, as a final resting- place for those who here gave their lives, that that nation might live.
>
> It is altogether fitting and proper that we should do this.
>
> But, in a larger sense, we cannot dedicate, we cannot consecrate- we cannot hallow- this ground. The brave men, living and dead, who struggled here, have consecrated it far above our poor power to add or detract.
>
> The world will little note, nor long remember what we say here, but it can never forget what they did here.

It is for us the living, rather, to be dedicated here to the unfinished work which they who fought here have thus far so nobly advanced. It is rather for us here to be dedicated to the great task remaining before us- that from these honored dead we take increased devotion to that cause for which they here gave the last full measure of devotion—that we here highly resolve that these dead shall not have died in vain—that this nation, under God, shall have a new birth of freedom, and that government of the people, by the people, for the people, shall not perish from the earth."

The Civil War would continue for more than sixteen months after Lincoln's famous speech, but the Gettysburg Address was a huge moment for freedom for all in the United States. Lincoln had also issued an executive order called the Emancipation Proclamation effective January 1, 1863, declaring all enslaved people in the Confederate States to be "forever free."

Historians estimate that between 620,000 and 750,000 military members died as a result of the four years of bloodshed in the American Civil War, with some estimates being even higher. These numbers do not include civilian casualties. More than 60 percent of the deaths were due to disease rather than battle. Over 360,000 deaths were on the Union side—more than 17 percent of the 2.1 million who enlisted. Of the nearly 200,000 Black soldiers enlisted for the Union, roughly 20 percent died in battle or by disease.

The fight for freedom for all did not come easily or without a heavy price. Tremendous losses came on the battlefields, and the most powerful figure behind the abolition of slavery, Abraham Lincoln, was assassinated. Lincoln was shot on April 14, 1865, just five days after the Civil War ended, at Ford's Theatre in Washington, DC, by a famous actor and Confederate sympathizer named John Wilkes Booth. The sixteenth president died of his wounds the next day.

★ ★ ★

The most important thing we can do as Americans is learn from past mistakes and injustices, come together and move forward as one nation. There is not a country in the world that doesn't have past or present injustices, and what was considered normal *yesterday* often is not *today*. Atrocities against Native Americans and slavery are the two most glaring injustices in American History, but it is not logical to use these or any other past injustices to tear down a government and replace it with one that gives its citizens fewer rights or opportunities. American democracy was set up to work. It was set up with the checks and balances of three branches of government, the power was given to the people with their right to vote and the laws to be upheld or struck down by the Supreme Court, thus protecting the Constitution.

Chapter Four

Would it be too much to ask for a century of peace? The 1900s came and sadly, so did horrendous crimes against humanity responsible for the deaths of tens of millions of people throughout the world. The United States was forced into World War II after the then-totalitarian country of Japan attacked our naval base at Pearl Harbor on December 7, 1941.

We have all heard about Pearl Harbor. Most people know a bit about the surprise attack on our naval base located in Hawaii, officially bringing the United States into WWII. Not as many, however, under-stand what had been happening in the Far East in the years leading up to the attack.

In 1937, a year after signing a pact with Nazi Germany, Japan abolished all of their elections. That same year, they attacked China, starting an undeclared and very long war. Their goal was Japanese dominance over most of Eastern Asia and the Pacific, often referred to as the Greater East Asia Co-Prosperity Sphere. This objective had to be achieved through conquering those countries that did not share the beliefs of Japanese dominance. Their ideals were totalitarian, anti-Western, and based on propaganda. The main theology of the Greater East Asia Co-Prosperity Sphere was superiority of the Japanese race over all other Asians. Political and military leaders in Japan knew that acquiring more territory would give them more resources, power and control.

No areas of society in Imperial Japan were free of censorship—including in the press. In September of 1937, a new censorship guideline for newspapers stated that any news article or photograph unfavorable to the Imperial Army would be subjected to a gag.

One atrocity and example of media censorship in Imperial Japan was the Nanking Massacre, often referred to as the Rape of Nanking. In December of 1937, five months after the Japanese invasion of China began, the Japanese Army captured Nanking, the Chinese capital. For six weeks, soldiers of the Imperial Japanese Army murdered tens of thousands of unarmed Chinese soldiers and civilians and committed widespread rape and looting. The estimates of those murdered and raped vary widely and go as high as 300,000 murdered and 80,000 women raped.

Japan imposed complete censorship of all materials covering or mentioning the Nanking Massacre. Those back home in Japan didn't read about the rape and murder or see photographs of the dead. There were, however, photographic records of the massacre, and high-ranking military personnel were later convicted of war crimes. Even to this day, some Japanese deny this massacre occurred.

The Cabinet Intelligence Bureau was founded in 1940, adding yet another blanket covering any freedoms related to free speech or thought in Imperial Japan. The Cabinet Intelligence Bureau had complete control over all news, advertising and public events. Rather than tell the truth or report the facts, the media was used to win ideological warfare or defeat an opponent's ideology. Sound familiar?! Writers were blacklisted and airwaves were controlled by the Japanese government.

Fast-forward to the present and the scariest part of this decade hasn't been the outbreak of Covid, riots, or increased crime, but rather propaganda, censorship of voices and increased government control.

The First Amendment to the US Constitution gives the American people the right to free speech, allowing us to be heard without fear of being silenced or persecuted. Freedom of speech is something we have been afforded that those in the Imperial Japanese Empire did not have in the decade leading up to or during WWII.

★ ★ ★

Through the Lend-Lease Act and economic sanctions that were placed on the Axis powers of Japan, Germany, and Italy, the United States had been indirectly involved in World War II for over two years before the December 1941 attack on Pearl Harbor. After Pearl Harbor, the US immediately declared war on the Axis powers which started our direct military involvement.

Pearl Harbor was a surprise attack to most of the world, but the Japanese had officially been preparing for almost a year. The plans began eleven months prior in January of 1941 and were masterminded by Admiral Yamamoto. Yamamoto had attended Harvard University (yes, that Harvard!) from 1919 to 1921, where he studied English and American culture. He later returned to the United States from 1926 to 1928 as a naval attaché in Washington.

American intelligence broke a Japanese code giving up Yamamoto's location in April 1943, and a small fleet of American fighters flew to intercept the Admiral's small fleet. Yamamoto's plane was shot down by American *P-38s* over the island of Bougainville in Papua New Guinea. The Admiral's plane crashed in the jungle, although it was determined that he died before the crash due to rounds fired from the attack. The mission was named Operation Vengeance.

★★★

Yamamoto's history is one example of the dishonesty or ignorance of so many on the left who claim the United States is an intolerant, racist nation. Throughout history, the United States has let many enemies inside its borders, a main reason being just how tolerant of a country America is and has been. It happened with Yamamoto before the Second World War, just as it happened seventy-five years later with the terrorists responsible for the 9/11 attacks. The same Al Qaeda terrorists who had attended flight school right here in the US, remember?

In the summer of 2020, congresswoman Ilhan Omar of Minnesota's 5th District said:

> "As long as our economy and political systems prioritize profit without considering who is profiting, who is being shut out, we will perpetuate this inequality. So we cannot stop at [the] criminal justice system. We must begin the work of dismantling the whole system of oppression wherever we find it."

What system of oppression is Omar talking about? The same one that granted her family asylum when they fled their home country of Somalia, granted her citizenship within five years, and elected her to the US House of Representatives multiple times? So, there wasn't opportunity for Omar in the United States? She is just one of unlimited examples of America-hating far leftists who show their dishonesty and/or ignorance. Is it possible to be more hypocritical?

Furthermore, it needs to be asked what Omar's quote infers. Which areas of society does she want to dismantle? Does she want to dismantle American society entirely? I think the answer is clear.

★★★

Pearl Harbor was one of many brutal and unnecessary attacks or invasions that happened on the "day that will live in infamy." That same day, the Philippines, Hong Kong, Guam, Wake Island and Malaya were also victims of Japanese invasions. In the next several months, Japan invaded Burma, Java, Borneo, Thailand, Singapore and the Aleutian Islands as well. In many places such as the Philippines, the Japanese forces took control of the country, but many groups and individuals refused to give up their weapons and fought as guerillas until Allied liberation in the later years of the war.

The Pacific theater is usually overshadowed in most history classes and documentaries by the atrocities of Nazi Germany simultaneously happening in Europe. Though very often overshadowed, the atrocities of Japan were comparable to those of Nazi Germany. These occurred throughout a large portion of the Pacific and much of eastern and southeastern Asia, with the Chinese having by far the most civilian casualties. Many books have been written about these Japanese abominations and war crimes, including the one best known to Americans: the Bataan Death March.

★ ★ ★

The designed Japanese attacks and invasions in December of 1941 spanned much of the Pacific and Southeast Asia, from Honolulu to Sumatra. The Philippines was not spared, either, as a Japanese invasion force of over 120,000 ground troops landed on the island nation within the first three weeks of the invasion. Brutal jungle fighting took place for over five months with the starving and exhausted American and Filipino troops trying to fend off their attackers.

While the continuous fighting in the Philippines raged on from December 1941 to May 1942, the Americans were continually shocked by the brutality and savagery of the Japanese. No rules of war were followed, as the Japanese would kill medics, babies, or civilians with no hesitation!

The surrender of Bataan on April 9, 1942, by General King marked the beginning of what would become known as the Bataan Death March. The Bataan Death March was the brutal eighty-mile trek to the O'Donnell prison camp of some 75,000 to 80,000 bewildered, beaten, starved and sick Americans and Filipinos. The prisoners were taunted, starved, beaten, stabbed, shot and sometimes beheaded along the march by their Japanese captors. Anyone who asked for water would be killed.

Over 10,000 of the Americans and Filipinos died along the march as well as another 22,000 at Camp O'Donnell. Thousands of Filipinos and a much smaller number of Americans were able to escape the Death March. Many of the Filipinos who escaped returned to their homes and blended back into society, while others became guerillas and, alongside escaped Americans, fought the Japanese until liberation by the General MacArthur- led American forces in late 1944 and early 1945.

★ ★ ★

Thousands of Japanese came into the Philippines at will in the years leading up to the December 1941 invasion. Many of them purchased land, bought into Filipino businesses and smuggled in more of their countrymen, who often claimed to be merchants, tourists, fisherman or bird fanciers.

As a very intelligent and educated man, current Florida Governor Ron DeSantis is aware of the dangers of foreign nations buying large amounts of US property. In July of 2022, DeSantis stated that those who have business interests with the Chinese Communist Party should not be allowed to buy up American real estate assets and that it isn't always apparent what Chinese companies in the US are doing.

Chinese investors, including those from Hong Kong and Taiwan, bought $6.1 billion in US real estate from April 2021 to March of 2022. Chinese companies are also buying large amounts of US farmland. In 2019, the US Department of Agriculture said that Chinese-linked enti-ties owned at least 192,000 acres of US farmland worth more than

$1.9 billion. In July 2022, the Chinese company Fufeng Group bought more than 300 acres of North Dakota farmland. Given the very close proximity to Grand Forks Air Force Base, which specializes in military drone technology, this is very concerning and needs to be monitored.

The US currently has no restrictions or citizenship requirements for real estate purchases by foreigners. It is tougher for a foreigner to get approved for financing, but cash transactions are easy. There are *many* more restrictions, of course, for foreigners to purchase property in China. These include the ability to only purchase residential property, the inability to be a landlord, a long-term visa requirement and the restriction of purchasing only one piece of property. The left has been somewhat successful in painting the utterly false narrative that the United States is an intolerant county when in fact, it has been one of the most tolerant and accepting countries on Earth—many times to its own detriment!

Border security is NOT racist!

★ ★ ★

One often takes their freedoms for granted until they are taken away. Those who have lived through a totalitarian regime understand this much better than most Americans do. Whether a right-wing or left-wing totalitarian regime, many personal freedoms are not permitted.

Tomás Confesor, a pre-WWII governor of the Philippine Province of Iloilo, was in Manilla when Japan attacked the Philippines on December 8, 1941. He was able to escape to the mountains of the Philippine island of Panay, where he led guerillas in resistance to the Japanese occupation. He said this:

> "There is a total war in which the issues between the warring parties are less concerned with territorial questions but more with forms of government, ways of life, and those that affect even the very thoughts, feelings and sentiments of every man. In other

words, the question at stake with respect to the Philippines is not whether Japan or the United States should possess it but more fundamentally it is: what system of government would stand here and what ways of life, system of social organization and code of morals should govern our existence....

You may not agree with me but the truth is that the present war is a blessing in disguise to our people and that the burden it imposes and the hardships it has brought upon us are a test of our character to determine the sincerity of our convictions and the integrity of our souls. In other words, this war has placed us in the crucible, to assay the metal in our beings. For as a people, we have been living during the last forty years under a regime of justice and liberty regulated only by universally accepted principles of constitutional governments. We have come to enjoy personal privileges and civil liberties without much struggle, without undergoing any pain to attain them. They were practically a gift from a generous and magnanimous people—the people of the United States of America. Now that Japan is attempting to destroy those liberties, should we not exert every effort to defend them? Should we not be willing to suffer for their defense? If our people are undergoing hardships now, we are doing it gladly, it is because we are willing to pay the price for those constitutional liberties and privileges. You cannot become wealthy by honest means without sweating heavily. You know very well that the principles of democracy and democratic institutions were brought to life through bloodshed and fire. If we sincerely believe in those principles and institutions, as we who are resisting Japan do, we should contribute to the utmost of our capacity to the cost of its maintenance to save them from destruction and annihilation and such contribution should be in terms of painful sacrifices, the same currency that other peoples paid for those principles."

The Filipino people generally hated the Japanese, and many tried to help the Americans. Many would feed the Americans who had escaped, house them, treat their wounds, or warn them of nearby Japanese troops. Many Americans temporarily ended up in the Fassoth camps, which got their name from Bill Fassoth, the owner of a 1,600-acre rice and sugar farm. In December 1941, soon after the war began, Japanese planes bombed his house, sugar mill, and rice mill and shot all his cows. He and his family retreated into the mountains. Their original intention was their own survival, but they ended up housing and healing dozens of escaped and wounded American soldiers.

On September 26, 1942, the Japanese found and invaded the camp. Men were butchered with bayonets. A baby started to cry, and one of the Japanese soldiers pulled it by its feet and then struck off its head with the slash of a sword. After the invaders killed or took the occupants prisoner, the camp was burned. The prisoners were taken to internment camps, where they were put in four-by-four-feet cages and were only taken out when tortured. They were interrogated, beaten with blackjacks or baseball bats, lit on fire, or had their hands clamped to a table and bamboo slits shoved under their fingernails.

Japanese Captain Yoshio Tsuneyoshi once told a group of American POWs, "We do not consider you to be prisoners of war. You are members of an inferior race, and we will treat you as we see fit. Whether you live or die is of no concern to us."

Even the injured Japanese soldiers did not escape the brutality of their countrymen. Often, the injured were killed to avoid slowing the pace of their military operations, and this was done by any means—including burning their injured men to death inside buildings.

★★★

The differences of attitude, brutality, treatment of prisoners and regard to human life between the Japanese and the Americans during WWII could not have been further apart. Given the Japanese generally fought to the death, there were very few POWs captured by the allies in the Pacific theater. The few who were captured were shipped to POW camps in Australia or New Zealand. Of course, the condition of any

POW camp is very unpleasant, , but the Japanese were not treated with anywhere close to the same brutality as those who had been captured by their countrymen. The Japanese POWS were able to paint, and they completed many works of art at the camps. If not killed, those imprisoned by the Japanese sometimes didn't leave with all of their fingers—forget the artwork.

Through control of the media, the totalitarian government of Imperial Japan passed on a plethora of lies to their people. Quite possibly the biggest lie was who the Americans actually were. Even though Japan was, in fact, the one responsible for massacres of civilians, attacks and invasions that led to the deaths of over 25 million people, most Japanese believed they were in the right, fighting for the emperor and country. They were told the American soldiers were killers and cannibals, and the Japanese were so terrified of capture that they fought to the death or committed suicide rather than surrender.

The propaganda fed to the Japanese about American soldiers could not have been further from the truth! Many of the WWII commanding officers were WWI veterans who were successful and stayed in the military. Most of those who enlisted or were drafted were young men who had spent their childhoods trying to make it through the daily struggle of the Great Depression and were happy to have a good meal or a quarter in their pocket. The young people during this time in history have rightly become known as the Greatest Generation due to their hard work, resilience, bravery, and determination to persevere through both the Great Depression and World War II.

Throughout the 1930s, these kids experienced a level of poverty that most today don't understand. According to the National WWII Museum, 61 percent of the U.S. military members were draftees and 39 percent volunteers. Many of these young men viewed the military as an opportunity to get out of the slums of the city or the dust of rural America.

★ ★ ★

Early on the morning of February 15, 1945, US patrol planes were scourging the western Pacific waters for any sign of the enemy. Two planes sighted and sank a small boat. The only survivor found was a seventeen-year-old Japanese boy named Sadao Watanabe. His leg had been broken by a bullet.

Sadao was taken aboard the aircraft carrier *USS Yorktown,* where he was given medical attention and food. When the food tray was placed on his knees, two peas rolled off the tray. Sadao was so hungry that he picked up those two fallen peas and ate them before he started eating the rest of the food on his plate. After the boy had eaten, he was questioned and remained on the carrier to recover. Despite being shot, he appreciated the kindness he received on the *Yorktown* and said he planned to enlist in the US Navy after his leg healed.

When the *Yorktown* returned to Ulithi on March 1, 1945, Sadao was sad when he was told he was being taken to a hospital on the island. He later sent two letters to the Yorktown—one to the pharmacist's mate who had taken care of him, and one to the entire crew. In the letter, Sadao thanked everyone and told them he hoped to be a crew member someday. The kindness of those of the *USS Yorktown* versus the brutality of Sadao's own countrymen indeed spoke volumes.

The name "Greatest Generation" became widespread after Tom Brokaw's book The Greatest Generation was published in 2000. *The Greatest Generation* refers to people born from the early 1900s through the late 1920s. It is also referred to as the GI Generation or the WWII Generation.

★ ★ ★

The fact that the Japanese were so willing to take on suicide missions and fight to die was hard for the young American men and boys to understand. The Americans had already had to fight to live through the Great Depression. Fighting to die for the emperor was the Japanese way, and this became even more the norm when they realized the war was lost.

Banzai charges were Japanese waves of suicide attacks in which their troops would scream and charge at Allied troops, not expecting to survive. They would often charge out from behind cover when the battle was near lost. The term *"banzai"* came from the phrase *"Tenno Heika Banzai,"* meaning "Long live His Majesty the Emperor." The largest banzai attack of WWII was during the battle of Saipan, where 4,300 Japanese soldiers attacked troops of the US Army and Marines. The American dead and wounded from the charge numbered nearly one thousand, and almost all the Japanese were killed.

The best-known suicide attack by the Japanese during World War II was, of course, the kamikaze. A "kamikaze" refers to a Japanese pilot during WWII who would make a deliberate suicidal crash on an Allied target, generally an aircraft carrier or another type of ship. The Japanese started their kamikaze attacks during the battle of Leyte Gulf in October 1944, under the belief that this tactic was the only way to stop the American offensive. These suicide attacks became more and more prevalent as the war continued. In the end, almost 4,000 kamikaze pilots died by this method.

★ ★ ★

While it was expected down the Japanese ranks to fight to die, the Americans fought to live. The United States invested a significant amount of manpower in caring for their sick and wounded. In a battalion of four hundred, roughly thirty were medics. During battle, the medics would stabilize the wounded and prepare them for evacuation to field hospitals. The US Navy and Marines had corpsmen. After passing their US Navy training, corpsmen would go to the Hospital Corps School where they learned first aid, anatomy and operations of medical equipment. After training, they would be assigned to US Navy hospitals, ships, or Navy Air Centers, and a select few would be sent to the Marines. Extensive medical treatment would generally have to wait until the wounded arrived at the field hospitals. The survivors were then sent to a hospital ship and finally a US Navy hospital for recovery.

Not only did America try to save lives with medical help and treatment of the wounded, but also with its war strategy. The United States incorporated a strategy in the Pacific known as "island hopping." Using this strategy, US troops would skip over Japanese occupied islands that were considered unnecessary or were predicted to result in too many casualties. The focus of island hopping was to take control of those islands of strategic importance, such as Saipan or Iwo Jima. The ultimate goal was not only to liberate the Pacific from their conquerors but also to get into position for the potential invasion of Japan if surrender was refused.

Lifelong Navy Commander and Rear Admiral Marc Mitscher was a prime example of an American commander trying to save lives. On June 20, 1944, the skies were alight during the second day of the First Battle of the Philippine Sea. Around 4:00 p.m. that day, a search plane spotted the Japanese fleet. Mitscher, who knew it would be dangerous launching an attack with nighttime approaching, hesitated but gave the order to launch. Planes started taking off from the carriers around 4:30. While en route to annihilate the enemy, it was discovered the Japanese carriers were sixty miles farther west than originally thought. These 120 additional miles made it certain the American planes would return after dark and would have to land on the carriers with no light, in addition to being low on fuel. Thus, the second wave of takeoffs was called off.

Around 6:30 p.m., the US Hellcats and Avengers spotted the Japanese fleet and lit it up. Bombs were dropped, the Japanese flagship carrier was damaged, another carrier was sunk and several other ships were badly damaged. The attack was a great success!

As the US planes headed back to their fleet, each pilot watched his fuel gauge—below them, the ocean was dark. To run out of fuel in the dark, over the ocean meant almost certain death. The American fleet had to keep their lights off or they would greatly risk giving up their location to the Japanese. A night landing on the carriers was near impossible in the dark. It took some luck to even find the fleet, and it was near impossible to see which ship was an aircraft carrier they could land on and which wasn't.

Mitscher directed the carriers toward the pilots. Finally, the planes approached the carriers- one by one, the planes ran out of fuel and dropped into the sea. Mitscher knew that something had to be done or most of his men would be killed. Slowly, he got up from his seat and gave the order, **"Turn on the lights."** Soon after, he gave another: **"Land on any carrier."** This decision by Mitscher endangered the lives of thousands of men aboard the ships for approximately two hundred pilots and airmen; Mitscher, however, had promised the pilots they would get back safely. Most pilots either landed on the carriers or were picked up safely from the ocean after having to land on the water. Thirty-eight of the forty planes launched from the *USS Yorktown* on June 20, 1944, made it back to the carriers!

ALL LIVES MATTER!

★ ★ ★

When most people think of WWII, the Holocaust, Nazis, D-Day, Pearl Harbor, or the atomic bomb are likely what first come to mind. What is not commonly known today is how tropical diseases in the jungles of the South Pacific ravaged the health of thousands of young men. Malaria, dysentery, beriberi, dengue fever, cholera, poison ivy and fungal infections plagued military personnel throughout the tropical Pacific region. The rate of malaria infection in the South Pacific Area of WWII was calculated at about 251 cases per 1,000 troops. During the Battle of Buna in New Guinea, the medical department estimated the casualties due to malaria outnumbered combat casualties by seven to ten times. Lieutenant General Robert Eichelberger, the US commander at Buna, said "disease was a surer and more deadly peril to us than enemy marksmanship. We had to whip the Japanese before the malarial mosquito whipped us."

★ ★ ★

As the Pacific War continued and the Americans closed in on Japan, the tactics of the Japanese became more and more desperate and suicidal. The kamikaze attacks increased, and the death tolls mounted. The Japanese troops were instructed and expected to fight to the death and take as many Americans as possible with them, and in no battle were more lives lost per square mile than on the western Pacific island of Iwo Jima. Iwo Jima sits some 750 miles south-southeast of Japan and was of great strategic importance to both the Japanese and the Americans.

The island only consisted of eight square miles or 4,850 acres, but it was fortified and guarded by over twenty-one thousand troops of the Japanese Army. Every foot of the island could be fired upon by the Japanese- through foxholes, machine gun nests, caves, pillboxes, bunkers or concrete emplacements. All Japanese fortifications were able to fire on each other. Thus, when the Marines took over one location, it would be fired upon by the next Japanese emplacement. Many of the Japanese remained underground and were never seen until the Marines were literally right on top of them. Underground caves and mazes of tunnels were honeycombed throughout the island, allowing the Japanese to carry out deadly surprise attacks.

One such surprise attack took place in the early morning hours of March 26, 1945. The airmen of 531st Squadron were among the many Americans attempting to rest that early morning on the rocky volcanic island covered in sand, ash and blood as they were anticipating the planned early morning takeoff to bomb the nearby island of Haha Jima. Around 4:00 a.m. that early morning, hundreds of Japanese started rising from their underground mazes, knowing the end was near. Yelling "Banzai!", the remaining Japanese on the island ran from cover to the American-occupied tents. The Americans fought off their enemies that early morning, but not before forty-four soldiers lost their lives and one hundred more were wounded. The island had prematurely and incorrectly been declared secure on March 16.

The iconic image most people remember from the Battle of Iwo Jima is of the six war heroes raising the American flag on Mount Suribachi, the island's highest point. This iconic piece of history occurred on February 23, 1945, just four days after the bloody battle began. The photograph that became famous was actually taken several hours after Marine photographer Louis Lowery captured Marines from the 28th Regiment of the 5th Division raising a smaller flag atop Mount Suribachi. There was a huge elated response from the Marines fighting below and the sailors offshore as the men cheered, and the ships' horns blew when they saw the initial raising of the American flag. It also brought increased Japanese gunfire to the top of the 554-foot mountain.

This caused Lowery to dive for cover and his camera to break during the fall. Due to the American boost in morale after the first flag was raised hours earlier, Lieutenant Colonel Chandler Johnson ordered a larger flag to be raised atop Mount Suribachi. This is when AP photographer Joe Rosenthal captured the image that became famous. The six men in Rosenthal's photo were thought for decades to be Corporal

Harlon Block, Navy Pharmacist's Mate John Bradley, Corporal Rene Gagnon, Private First Class Franklin Sousley, Sergeant Michael Strank, and Corporal Ira Hayes. In 2016, the Marine Corps made a statement that Private First Class Harold Schultz was in the photograph by Rosenthal. It was determined that Navy Pharmacist's Mate John Bradley took part in the initial flag raising but was not one of the six men in the second photo. Very sadly, three of these six brave men (Block, Sousley and Strank) were killed before the end of the battle.

Mount Suribachi is on the very southern end of the island, to the west of the southeast landing beaches. As mentioned, the Americans captured Mount Suribachi on the fourth day of the battle, but it would take several horrible weeks to secure the island. Foot by foot, through deadly resistance, the Marines moved north-northeast until the island was cleared of the enemy. The United States completely secured Iwo Jima after over five weeks of savage fighting. The victory did, however, come with a huge cost. Of the nearly 70,000 US landing forces, 6,821 were killed and 19,217 wounded. Of the deaths, 5,563 were US Marines. All but a few hundred of the more than 21,000 Japanese on the island were killed. After the fighting ceased, Iwo Jima was used as an emergency landing spot for US planes. More than 2,200 B-29 bombers landed on the little island's airstrips during the remainder of the war, potentially saving the lives of up to 24,000 airmen!

★ ★ ★

There was an even greater loss of life in the last large-scale battle of WWII: Okinawa. In over eleven weeks of fighting from April to June of 1945, almost 19,000 Americans lost their lives, while more than 100,000 Japanese soldiers and an estimated 80,000 to 100,000 civilians died. Japanese civilians who survived Okinawa disclosed that fanatical Japanese soldiers gave orders for the civilian population to commit suicide—a wicked betrayal of the Japanese people enabled by indoctrinations, lies and censorship by the Japanese government controlling the schools and the media!

"We were told that if women were taken prisoner we would be raped and we should not allow ourselves to be captured," said Sumie Oshiro, an Okinawa survivor, in 2007. Oshiro and three others had tried to kill themselves with a hand grenade to evade capture, but it didn't go off. Families committed suicide together, many jumping off cliffs to their deaths.

Sadly, less than eight decades later, indoctrination, propaganda, lies and belief in government command have swallowed up many in the United States of America—many whose fathers, grandfathers and great-grandfathers sacrificed so much fighting against the very same thing.

Due to the mounting casualties, brutality and extreme tactics of Japan, Allied commanders became increasingly worried about what it would take to end the war. How many lives would be lost with an invasion of the home islands, they asked? As the world soon found out, there was a possible alternative awaiting in the New Mexico desert.

★ ★ ★

The project of the development of the atomic bomb, called the Manhattan Project, was so top secret that Vice President Harry Truman was not aware it existed. Interestingly, when he was a senator in 1943, senatorial investigations led Truman to become aware of and ask questions regarding a plant in Pasco, Washington, that was part of the top-secret project. His inquiry led to a phone call from Secretary of War Henry Stimson, asking him not to investigate further.

After the death of FDR on April 12, 1945, Truman was informed of the Manhattan Project, and what was likely the biggest decision in history loomed before him. Given the barbarity of the Japanese and the extreme casualties on both sides later in the war, Truman was very hesitant of an invasion of the Japanese home islands. Truman and other Allied leaders met in Potsdam, Germany, in July of 1945, where the president addressed the Japanese refusal to surrender in his Potsdam Declaration:

> "We, the President of the United States, the President of the National Government of the Republic of China and the Prime Minister of Great Britain, representing the hundreds of millions of our countrymen, have conferred and agree that Japan shall be given an opportunity to end this war.

> The prodigious land, sea and air forces of the United States, the British Empire and of China, many times reinforced by their armies and air fleets from the west are poised to strike the final blows upon Japan. This military power is sustained and inspired by the determination of all the Allied nations to prosecute the war against Japan until she ceases to resist.

> The result of the futile and senseless German resistance to the might of the aroused free peoples of the world stands forth is awful clarity as an example to the people of Japan. The might that now converges upon Japan is immeasurably greater than that which, when applied to the resisting Nazis, necessarily laid waste to the lands, the industry and the method of life of the whole German people. The full application of our military power, backed by our resolve, will mean the inevitable and complete destruction of the Japanese armed forces and just as inevitably the utter devastation of the Japanese homeland.

> The time has come for Japan to decide whether she will continue to be controlled by those self-willed militaristic advisors whose unintelligent calculations have brought the Empire of Japan to the threshold of annihilation, or whether she will follow the path of reason.

> Following are our terms. We will not deviate from them. There are no alternatives.

There must be eliminated for all time the authority and influence of those who have deceived and misled the people of Japan into embarking on world conquest, for we insist that a new order of peace, security and justice will be impossible until irresponsible militarism is driven from the world.

Until such a new order is established *and* until there is convincing proof that Japan's war-making power is destroyed, points in Japanese territory to be designated by the Allies shall be occupied to secure the achievement of the basic objectives we are here setting forth.

The terms of the Cairo Declaration shall be carried out and Japanese sovereignty shall be limited to the islands of Honshu, Hokkaido, Kyushu, Shikoku and such minor islands as we determine.

The Japanese military forces, after being completely disarmed, shall be permitted to return to their homes with the opportunity to lead peaceful and productive lives.

We do not intend that the Japanese shall be enslaved as a race or destroyed as a nation, but stern justice shall be meted out to all war criminals, including those who have visited cruelties upon our prisoners. The Japanese government shall remove all obstacles to the revival and strengthening of democratic tendencies among the Japanese people. Freedom of speech, of religion, and of thought, as well as respect for the fundamental human rights shall be established.

Japan shall be permitted to maintain such industries as will sustain her economy and permit the exaction of just reparations in kind, but not those industries which would enable her to re-arm for war. To this end, access to, as distinguished from control of raw materials shall be permitted. Eventual Japanese participation in world trade relations shall be permitted.

The occupying forces of the Allies shall be withdrawn from Japan as soon as these objectives have been accomplished and there has been established in accordance with the freely expressed will of the Japanese people a peacefully inclined and responsible government.

We call upon the Government of Japan to proclaim now the uncon-
ditional surrender of all the Japanese armed forces, and to provide
proper and adequate assurances of their good faith in such action.
The alternative for Japan is prompt and utter destruction."

Japan initially rejected the Potsdam Declaration. On July 31, 1945,
Truman gave the ok to use the bomb- no sooner than August 2.

Around 2:45 a.m. on August 6, 1945, a B-29 bomber named *Enola
Gay*, flown by Colonel Paul Tibbets and navigated by Captain Theodore
Van Kirk, left Tinian Island. It flew north, rendezvoused with two other
bombers over Iwo Jima and the trio headed for the island of Honshu,
the largest of the Japanese islands. The cargo that day consisted of a
nine-thousand-pound atomic bomb nicknamed Little Boy. At 8:15 a.m.
Major Tom Ferebee pushed a lever in the bomb bay, and Little Boy was
dropped over its planned target of Hiroshima.

Hiroshima was leveled. There was still no response from Japan.

Three days later, on August 9, 1945, a second atomic bomb was
dropped over the Japanese city of Nagasaki. An estimated 130,000 to
215,000 people died between the two blasts, both immediately and
from long-term side effects. The loss of life was severe but just a small
fraction of what it would have been had there been an invasion of the
Japanese home islands.

After much debate, Emperor Hirohito finally agreed to a proposal
by Prime Minister Suzuki in which Japan would accept the Potsdam
Declaration. At noon on August 15, 1945, Emperor Hirohito went on
national radio to announce the Japanese surrender.

**Many high-ranking Japanese officials and members of the Imperial
Guard did not want to surrender and attempted a coup on August 14 and 15
1945 with the goal of placing Emperor Hirohito on house arrest. The coup
ultimately failed, and those attempting it committed suicide.**

★ ★ ★

By the summer of 1945, Japan was unquestionably defeated, yet still refused to surrender. Their navy, air force, and means of production were destroyed, but they still had around two million soldiers and 75 million civilians on the home islands, most of whom would have fought to the death or committed suicide as they had during previous battles. The United States valued life and gave Japan plenty of time and opportunity to surrender before the new weapon was used. The totalitarian government of Japan, however, did not have compassion for the loss of life or hold the best interest of the Japanese people!

The Americans dropped millions of leaflets, known as the LeMay leaflets, over Japanese cities to warn the civilian population of the power of the atomic bomb and encourage them to petition their leaders to surrender. The leaflets were written in Japanese, and there were at least three versions. The first version was dropped in the days leading up to Hiroshima and the other two in the days afterwards. They were designed by and got their name from General Curtis LeMay. This is the text of one of the leaflets dropped in between the Hiroshima and Nagasaki blasts, which was declassified in 1990:

To The Japanese People:

America asks that you take immediate heed of what we say on this leaflet.

We are in possession of the most destructive explosive ever devised by man. A single one of our newly developed atomic bombs is actually the equivalent in explosive power to what 2000 of our giant B-29s can carry on a single mission. This awful fact is one for you to ponder and we solemnly assure you it is grimly accurate.

We have just begun to use this weapon against your homeland. If you still have any doubt, make inquiry as to what happened to Hiroshima when just one atomic bomb fell on that city.

Before using this bomb to destroy every resource of the military by which they are prolonging this useless war, we ask that you now petition the Emperor to end the war. Our President has outlined for you the thirteen consequences of an honorable surrender. We urge that you accept these consequences and begin the work of building a new, better and peace- loving Japan.

You should take steps now to cease military resistance. Otherwise, we shall resolutely employ this bomb and all our other superior weapons to promptly and forcefully end the war.

EVACUATE YOUR CITIES.

This is a radio message from Harry Truman between the atomic blasts, around August 8, 1945:

"The British, Chinese and the United States Governments have given the Japanese people adequate warning of what is in store for them. We have laid down the general terms on which they can surrender. Our warning went unheeded; our terms were rejected. Since then, the Japanese have seen what our atomic bomb can do. They can foresee what it will do in the future. [. . .]

Having found the bomb we have used it. We have used it against those who attacked us without warning at Pearl Harbor, against those who have starved and beaten and executed American prisoners of war, against those who have abandoned all pretense of obeying international laws of warfare. We have used it in order to shorten the agony of war, in order to save the lives of thousands and thousands of young Americans.

We shall continue to use it until we completely destroy Japan's power to make war. Only a Japanese surrender will stop us."

During the deadliest war in history, while using the deadliest weapon ever developed at that time, the United States had concern for human life. Can anyone imagine what would have happened if the bomb had fallen into Japanese or German hands in the early 1940s?

With his decision to use the atomic bomb, Harry Truman very likely saved the lives of 1.5 to 2 million Americans and tens of millions of Japanese. An invasion of the Japanese home islands would have been catastrophic!

★ ★ ★

World War II officially ended on September 2, 1945, when the surrender was signed on the Battleship *Missouri* in Tokyo Bay. General MacArthur, who President Truman had just assigned the task of rebuilding Japan, said this on that day:

> "It is my earnest hope, and indeed the hope of all mankind, that from this solemn occasion a better world shall emerge out of the blood and carnage of the past, a world founded upon faith and understanding, a world dedicated to the dignity of man and the fulfillment of his most cherished wish for freedom, tolerance and justice."

These signatures in Tokyo Bay marked a huge defeat for totalitarianism and a huge win for global freedom! The two deadliest wars in American History were fought against slavery and totalitarianism, leading to the freedom and future freedoms of hundreds of millions of people!

★ ★ ★

The Allied occupation of Japan lasted from the end of World War II in 1945 until April of 1952. Overseen by General MacArthur, a Conservative man, the main goals were to eliminate Japan's potential to wage war and build its government into a democracy. All forms of Japanese censorship and restrictions on freedom of speech were immediately abolished. MacArthur immediately set up a food distribution network to feed the starving population. The war had been devastating to the Japanese people, and most of the country was starving.

The new Japanese constitution went into effect in May of 1947. This mandated a bill of rights, granted fair elections with the right to vote, outlawed Japan from making war and stripped Emperor Hirohito of all but symbolic power. Three branches of government were created, the legislative branch being bicameral—very similar to the US model.

Many of the rich landowners in Japan had supported the war expansionism and the censorship of the Japanese people. MacArthur knew land reform was needed, and almost 40 percent of cultivated land was bought from the landowners and sold to the tenants at a low cost. The Supreme Commander helped to create small businesses, grow free-market capitalism and break up the large business conglomerates in Japan.

Those who possibly benefited most from the new government of Japan were the women. Japanese wives had been expected to be obedient, passive and were expected to stop working for wages upon marriage. General MacArthur directed the committee drafting the new Japanese constitution to outlaw gender discrimination. Japanese women were then allowed greater freedoms, equality toward men, higher status in Japanese society, the ability to marry whom they chose and the right to vote!

This is a statement from General MacArthur in June of 1946 on the new role of women in Japanese society:

"Women of Japan are responding magnificently to the challenge of democracy; their record of participation in the general elections on 10 April sets an example for the world.

Japanese women are displaying an increasing interest in political, social, and economic affairs which exceeds the most hopeful anticipation of political observers. It attests to the powerful appeal of the democratic idea and to the enthusiasm with which Japanese women are discarding the age-old bonds of convention which have

so long denied them the fundamental democratic right to participate in communal affairs beyond the home."

Douglas MacArthur became quite popular and admired by the Japanese people during his time as the commander rebuilding their nation. They referred to him as the "Gentle Conqueror." Thousands would gather each day to watch him come and go from the Dai Ichi Building, where he worked in Tokyo. The US occupation of Japan officially ended in April of 1952 with the Treaty of San Francisco. It was a highly successful occupation completed with amazing speed!

★ ★ ★

Today, Japan has the third largest economy in the world. It is the birthplace of several inventions, such as Nintendo and PlayStation gaming consoles, created through free-market capitalism. Since the release of the Covid vaccine, many countries have imposed mandates related to vaccination status. Japan, the host of the 2021 Olympics, has not, but as of late 2021, they did have one of the highest vaccination rates in the world. Its health ministry "discourages discrimination against the unvaccinated and shot requirements in the workplace," and the Japanese ministry has stated, "Even if your company asks you to get vaccinated, you can choose not to if you do not want to."

Post-WWII Japan is a great historical example that shows what incredible contrast a people can make with some basic liberties. Japan quickly transformed from a barbaric, totalitarian country to a peace-loving, creative and very successful democracy! In less than a generation after WWII ended, Japan went from America's bitter enemy to trusted ally. This bears the question: Why can't we heal relationships within the United States?

General Douglas MacArthur (front left)

★ ★ ★

These are the final words by President Truman in his Recommendation for Assistance to Greece and Turkey as he addressed a joint session of Congress in March of 1947:

> "The United States contributed $341,000,000,000 toward winning World War II. This is an investment in world freedom and world peace.
>
> The assistance that I am recommending for Greece and Turkey amounts to little more than one-tenth of one percent of this investment. It is only common sense that we should safeguard this investment and make sure that it was not in vain.
>
> The seeds to totalitarian regimes are nurtured by misery and want. They spread and grow in the evil soil of poverty and strife. They reach their full growth when the hope of a people for a better life has died.
>
> We must keep that hope alive.

The free peoples of the world look to us for support in maintaining their freedoms.

If we falter in our leadership, we may endanger the peace of the world—and we shall surely endanger the welfare of our own Nation.

Great responsibilities have been placed upon us by the swift movement of events.

I am confident that the Congress will face these responsibilities squarely."

Truman was fearful of the "domino effect," or the idea that if one country fell under Communist influence or control, its neighboring countries would soon follow. His above address to Congress became the precedent of the United States for the following decades—doing whatever was necessary to contain the spread of Communism around the world, either economically or militarily.

Four months later, in July of 1947, President Truman signed into law the National Security Act that created the Department of Defense, the National Security Council, and the Central Intelligence Agency. The National Security Council (NSC) is based in the White House with its job to analyze intelligence and diplomatic information and provide the president reports of what was found. The role of the Central Intelligence Agency (CIA) is to gather intelligence and carry out covert operations in foreign nations.

Truman's policies were successful early on and helped tens of millions of people across the globe retain their freedoms. They did, however, lead to US involvement in the Korean and Vietnam wars, which cost us almost one hundred thousand American lives and hundreds of billions of dollars over three decades. These policies also increased the size of the federal government, which has only continued to get larger and larger.

Harry Truman

In July of 1948, Truman issued Executive Order 9981, desegregating and establishing equality and opportunity for all persons in the armed services without regard to race, color, religion or national origin. His influence helped persuade Congress to pass legislation almost doubling the minimum wage from $0.40/hour to $0.75/hour, which took effect in January of 1950. He also extended Social Security and gave federal assistance to farmers. Truman was president from April of 1945 to January of 1953, a very prosperous time in American history.

Ilhan Omar attended and graduated from college at North Dakota State University. From the start of 2019 through September of 2020, nearly $2.8 million of Omar's campaign funds were funneled to her husband Tim Mynett's political consulting company. These funds reportedly accounted for 80 percent of his company's income in 2020. After this was exposed in November of 2020, Omar allegedly cut ties with her husband's company. (Laughing emoji.) Mynett is Omar's third husband.

When the Korean War broke out in June of 1950, General MacArthur was selected to command that force as well as continue to oversee the occupation of Japan. The Korean War had some major successes, but in April of 1951, President Truman relieved MacArthur of both commands due to the general not following the orders of the president. This greatly upset the people of Japan, and two million Japanese showed up to bid MacArthur farewell days later when the general departed.

Chapter Five

The fight against Communism has not been an easy one. The philosophy of Communism derived from the writing of Karl Marx and Friedrich Engels known as *The Communist Manifesto*. This pamphlet, published in 1848, claimed that social classes were to blame for society's problems and called for a revolution by the working class, hoping to destroy capitalism.

The idea of Communism is appealing to some due to their desire for wealth re-distribution or free healthcare, no matter how bad the service may be. Others are simply willing to give their freedoms to the government in exchange for assistance. In the United States, the "capitalism versus socialism" debate in recent years has been a fight of ideologies. However, the key word is not "capitalism" or "socialism," but rather "totalitarianism."

When the government controls all facets of our lives—the economy, the schools, the healthcare system, medical choice, freedom of religion and speech, etc.-- we no longer live in a free country, but rather a totalitarian one. This is true in any extreme system of government, far right or far left. In the United States today, the far left is the ideology that is trying to take away our freedoms and pushing propaganda to do so. Politicians and figureheads on the American far left today are full of promises of entitlements they say are "free," such as direct income, free healthcare or free college tuition. The truth is, THESE ARE NOT FREE—either in dollars or in loss of freedoms!

★ ★ ★

Korea, which had been under Japanese rule since 1910, was divided into two occupation zones after World War II, as agreed at the Yalta Conference. The northern part of Korea would be controlled by the USSR and the southern part controlled by the United States. In 1947, the United States and Great Britain called for free elections throughout Korea, but the Soviet Union refused. In May of 1948, a Communist government called the Korean Democratic People's Republic was established in North Korea and in August of the same year, a democracy called the Democratic Republic of Korea was established in South Korea. The Korean War broke out two years later, and Korea remains divided to this day.

The Korean War began in June of 1950 when seventy-five thousand soldiers of the North Korean People's Army invaded South Korea, crossing the 38th parallel. Wanting to protect the free peoples of the world and fearing the spread of Communism, the United States immediately responded and sent troops to stop the North Korean Army.

> "If we let Korea down, the Soviets will keep right on going and swallow up one place after another."
>
> —Harry Truman, June 1950

Communist China* entered the war and sent troops in October of 1950 to help the North Koreans. The United States forces were successful in pushing the North Korean Army back across the 38th parallel by May of 1951, and the fighting remained in that vicinity until the end of the war. Finally, after two years of negotiations, an armistice was signed in July of 1953, ending the war and re-establishing the 1945 division of Korea.

★ ★ ★

Seven decades later, North Korea and South Korea could not be more different! The economy of North Korea is controlled by the government, which is unable to meet the basic needs of its people. The Kim family has been in power since 1948 and has prioritized themselves and their desire to develop nuclear weapons over the North Korean people. With the North Korean government controlling the means of production and distribution, it is tough to determine the country's exact economic data due to unreliable or nonexistent data. It is estimated, however, that its neighbor to the south has a GDP almost fifty times higher per capita than its own! According to worldpopulationreview. com, the GDP per capita is $31,617 in South Korea and $640 in North Korea! In total GDP, South Korea ranks tenth in the world as of 2022.

Amenities that we take for granted in the United States are not enjoyed in North Korea. According to the World Bank, more than half of North Koreans lacked access to electricity as recently as 2017!

China fell to Communism in late 1949 as the nationalist Chinese fled mainland China and took refuge in Taiwan. The nationalist and Communist Chinese had been in a civil war from 1946 to 1949.

Gross domestic product (GDP) is the total monetary or market value of all the finished goods and services produced within a country's borders in a specific time period. As a broad measure of overall domestic production, it functions as a comprehensive scorecard of a given country's economic health.

Per capita GDP measures a country's economic output per person and is calculated by dividing the GDP of a country by its population.

Not only do North Koreans lack adequate food and electricity, but also personal freedoms. Rather than having access to the World Wide Web, North Korea has its own internet network that has strict rules and doesn't allow users to access content from the rest of the world. Jacob Laukaitis, a travel blogger who visited both North and South Korea, said this:

> "Why were the people in the North not allowed to freely interact and share their thoughts with me, while the people in the South could do whatever the heck they wanted? Seeing these differences firsthand broke my heart. Why has life become so different for the Korean people in just a few generations?"

The answer is simple. One country has freedoms and rewards production, and the other one doesn't!

Mr. Laukaitis observed that the South Korean landscape was more lush and green, its residents gathered happily in parks and he noticed the parking lot of an amusement park was full. In contrast, he observed that the parking lots and roads in North Korea were much emptier.

★ ★ ★

> "Not Communism or Marxism is our idea. Our political philosophy is representative democracy and social justice in a well-planned economy."

Sound familiar…?! This quote—which sounds like it came from a Progressive leftist in the 2020s—was actually said by Fidel Castro when he spoke about the Cuban Revolution in 1953.

Castro promised free elections within eighteen months and told the people their property would not be seized. All of this, of course, turned out to be lies! In 1959, after Castro and his revolutionary guerillas took over Cuba, he quickly aligned with Communism. Private lands and bank accounts were seized by the Cuban government without due process, and the free elections he promised never happened. The Cuban Communist Party was officially founded in 1965 and all other political parties were banned, a ruling that was retained in constitutional referendums in both 1976 and 2002. Castro, himself, held the three highest political leadership positions in the country; head of state, head of government, and first secretary of the party. He was very polarizing and feared in Cuba.

Castro did deliver on his promise of free healthcare. Free, but not quality! Often, there was not enough money for supplies, multiyear waits for treatments and a lack of doctors. Like everyone in Cuba, its doctors are controlled by the government, and over time many of the best Cuban doctors have been sent to countries in Central or South America in exchange for natural resources, such as a doctor being sent to Venezuela in exchange for oil. In contrast to what many on the left think or want to believe, there are still social classes under socialism and Communism—two, actually. One for the elites, and one for everyone else. The health care system in Cuba is a perfect example, as it has two tiers: one tier for elites, tourists, and the military, and the other for everyone else. When people from the general population go to hospitals, they have to bring their own food, water, bed sheets and pillows.

Political prisoners have also been common in Cuba, and the education system does not tolerate critical thinking. Fidel Castro was the dictator of Cuba from 1959 until 2008, at which time he handed the power to his younger brother Raúl.

★ ★ ★

The fight against Communism continued with the Vietnam War. The long and controversial US involvement in Vietnam lasted two full decades, with the majority of the fighting taking place between 1965 and 1972. Saigon, the capital of South Vietnam, ultimately fell to the Vietcong on April 30, 1975, and the country became the Socialist

Republic of Vietnam in 1976. Vietnam is one of five Communist countries in the world today along with North Korea, Cuba, China and Laos.

★ ★ ★

Venezuela had the fourth highest per capita GDP in the world in 1950 and remained the wealthiest country in Latin America until the 1980s. In the 1970s, Venezuelan workers had the highest wages in Latin America! So, how did this once-booming economy go from being ranked the fourth highest GDP in the world in 1950 to 143rd in 2020?

Well, two things tanked the economy and the quality of life in Venezuela: the falling price of oil—its major natural resource that accounted for 95 percent of its exports—and the rise of socialism. The prior happened in the 1980s, and the latter in the 1990s.

In 1998, a former lieutenant colonel in the Venezuelan Army who had led a failed coup against the government in 1992 ran for president. His name was Hugo Chavez. After the attempted coup, Chavez was released from prison after only two years. He traveled to Cuba shortly afterward, where he made very positive remarks about socialism. He said this to Fidel Castro and the Cuban Parliament: "I do not deserve this honor. I hope I will deserve it one day. We are committed to the revolutionary work."

During his run for the presidency, Chavez downplayed his radicalism, saying he was neither for capitalism or socialism but a balance between the two. Frighteningly similar to those of the left in the United States today, he promised free government healthcare, free college education, social justice, and reduction of inequality. Chavez won the 1998 election.

Chavez did reduce inequality at first, but he made many radical changes that drastically hurt Venezuela. After several Venezuelan Supreme Court decisions went against Chavez's liking, he signed a court-packing law that allowed him to appoint twelve new justices. He also began to work on rewriting the Constitution, telling the Venezuelan Congress in 1999: "The constitution, and with it the ill-fated political system to which it gave birth 40 years ago, has to die. It is going to die, sirs—accept it."

Remember, he's talking about the same political system that was in effect while Venezuela was the most prosperous country in Latin America!

Hugo Chavez won re-election in 2006 on a socialist platform, this time with control of the legislature and the Supreme Court. At this point, private property was seized and private businesses, including media outlets and grocery stores, were nationalized. After the grocery stores were nationalized, people were put on food rations. The businesses that weren't nationalized were regulated by price controls, which led to many closing because they were no longer able to make a profit.

Inflation has continued to soar in Venezuela, to the point that someone making minimum wage today pays close to a quarter of their monthly wages on a liter of milk! Yes, one liter of milk!! As of 2017, it was estimated that 87 percent of Venezuelans lived in poverty and 64 percent had lost an average of over twenty-four pounds that year alone! Crime has skyrocketed, with the number of murders increasing by five times between 1999 and 2011 according to nongovernmental sources. Crime increased even more after the Control of Arms, Munitions and Disarmament Law went into effect in 2013, with the number of homicides increasing by an estimated additional 50 percent from 2011 to 2015. Many pro-democracy protests have taken to the streets in Venezuela only to be stopped by live ammunition and other forms of lethal force. From April 2017 to April 2018, at least 163 pro-democracy protesters in Venezuela were killed by the Maduro* dictatorship.

Vice President Nicolás Maduro took over the presidency after Chavez died in March of 2013.

Unsurprisingly, many Venezuelans have fled to other countries due to the government control, shortages, massive inflation and high crime. According to the United Nations, 5.6 million Venezuelans have left the country since 2014, with the majority moving to Columbia, Ecuador, Peru and Chile. This immigration accounts for roughly 20 percent of the current Venezuelan population of 28.5 million.

> "They stole these 20 years of life from all Venezuelans. They gave us a poor quality of life, they prevented us from having many professional opportunities and with them, they made Venezuela not advance but recede in all aspects: social, economic, industrial, educational, university."

> —Computer Engineering Professor in Western Venezuela

★ ★ ★

The Biden Administration eased restrictions on Cuba and sanctions on Venezuela in May of 2021. With regard to Cuba, the administration ended restrictions that limited the amount of money that people in the US were able to send to the island nation in addition to easing travel restrictions. Many people, including some Democrats, are skeptical of these policies. Val Demings, who ran against Marco Rubio for US senator in the November 2022 midterms, said, "Allowing investments in the Cuban private sector and easing travel restrictions will only serve to fund the corrupt dictatorship." Regarding Venezuela, the Biden Administration eased sanctions that will allow potential business dealings, such as the oil company Chevron to begin talks with Venezuela, regarding restarting oil production there. So why do you want to restrict (or eliminate) US oil production, Joe?

The problem with doing business with totalitarian governments is that the money doesn't get back to the people. The corrupt governments get richer, and the majority of the people remain dirt-poor! How have we not figured this out yet?! Yet so many in America are fighting (and voting) for the policies in those countries instead of the ones that have made our own country one of the most prosperous on Earth!

It is scary to think about the similar political ideologies, promises, and actions of Hugo Chavez a couple decades ago and those of the Progressive left today. Since the Biden Administration has taken office, we have seen the highest inflation in decades (by far), supply chain issues leading to empty shelves of essential products, the federal government threatening to weaponize the Department of Justice (the FBI) and a committee looking into adding justices to the Supreme Court. Sound familiar...?

★ ★ ★

Given the history of the last few decades in Cuba and Venezuela, the massive shift to the right among Cuban and Venezuelan voters should come as no surprise. As of 2020, 58 percent of registered Cuban voters say they affiliate or lean toward the Republican Party while 38 percent affiliate or lean toward the Democratic Party. In 2013, 47 percent identified or leaned Republican and 44 percent Democrat—a shift of 11 points in less than a decade!

The city of Doral, Florida, located in Miami-Dade County, had a population of just over sixty thousand in 2020. Over 72 percent of Doral's residents are Hispanic. In the 2020 presidential election, Donald Trump won the city by 1.4 points after having lost it by 40 points just four years earlier. In Miami-Dade County as a whole, Trump received a total of 532,833 votes—an increase of almost 200,000 from the 333,999 he received just four years prior. Meanwhile, Joe Biden received over 6,000 fewer votes from the 624,146 Hillary Clinton received in 2016. This shrunk the presidential margin of victory the Democrats had in Miami-Dade County from 30 points to 7 points in just four years!

In addition, Democratic incumbents from the 26th and 27th US

House Districts located in southern Florida were defeated in 2020 by Republican challengers. Not only are Republicans gaining more support from Cubans and Venezuelans, but also from Nicaraguans, Columbians, and Peruvians, with these voter demographics swinging 5 to 10 points to the right in the last decade.

Miami Dade County (Total Votes)

Year	Trump Votes	Clinton/Biden Votes
2016	333,999	624,146
2020	532,833	617,864

The Governor of Florida, Ron DeSantis, is even more popular among Cuban Americans than Trump, having received 66 percent of their vote statewide in the 2018 governor's election (compared to Trump's 56 percent in Florida in 2020). This support for Governor DeSantis likely will only increase given his strong support for both the people living in Cuba and for Cuban Americans. The following is a July 2021 statement from DeSantis, regarding the protests against the ruling Communist party in Cuba:

> "We stand with the people of Cuba. For far too long, a tyrannical communist regime has oppressed its people and used its power to silence any dissidents. Now, the Cuban people are making their voices heard to demand freedom and an end to this dictatorship.
>
> Still, while the Cuban people are showing tremendous courage, the Biden Administration is showing cowardice. The Biden Administration has been weak in its statements, blaming Covid-19 and not mentioning socialism or communism."

It was laughable to hear the Biden Administration's stance in the summer of 2021 regarding Cuban immigrants attempting to come to America to seek asylum. The protests against the Cuban government began on July 11, 2021, and shortly afterward, Homeland Security Director Alejandro Mayorkas said:

> "Allow me to be clear: If you take to the Sea, you will not come to the United States […] Again, I repeat: do not risk your life attempting to enter the United States illegally. You will not come to the United States."

Eye-opening, how quickly the Biden Administration spoke out against Cuban immigration, given how chaotic and open they have allowed the US southern border with Mexico to become! In the twelve full calendar months following Joe Biden's inauguration as president from February 2021 to January 2022, Border Patrol encountered a record **2,112,055** migrants at the southern border—well over double the 900,080 encounters from February 2019 to January of 2020. In 2021, the US Coast Guard encountered **838** Cubans attempting to make it to the US by sea the entire year—one individual for every 2,520 encountered at the US–Mexico border. So, why can't we accept Cuban refugees coming by sea, Alejandro?

Well, voting statistics may bring some clarity. While Cuban voters are more conservative, 65 percent of Hispanic voters nationally still identify with or lean toward the Democratic Party.

The protests in Cuba on July 11 and 12 of 2021 are believed to have led to more than one thousand arrests. Reuters reported speaking to many residents who said those who took part in the protests are now facing up to twenty-five years in prison. This is in a country where murderers receive eight to fifteen years! Cuban authorities, of course, will not comment.

The Republican Party did, however, gain popularity with Latino voters as a whole in most areas of the country between the 2016 and 2020 elections. This should not come as a surprise, given the large percentage of Hispanics who are working class and believe in the traditional family. From 2016 to 2020, Donald Trump made large gains among Hispanic voters in states such as Florida, Georgia, Nevada and Colorado and smaller gains in other states such as Texas and New York. Democrats had losses among Hispanic voters in the majority of states with the main exception being California. It seems likely that Hispanic voters will continue to trend to the right, which would be a huge boost in future elections.

★★★

Joe Biden has said many times he's "a capitalist, not a socialist." Eerily similar to Fidel Castro's message in 1953 and Hugo Chavez's message in the 1990s, Biden has repeatedly promised equity and social justice. He has downplayed how far to the left his policies are and has promised many *free* things from the central government. These *entitlements*, however, are not free!

Throughout his career as a Senator from Delaware, Biden has been against packing the Supreme Court. In 1983, while on the Senate Judiciary Committee, he said Franklin Roosevelt's proposal of packing the high court was a "bonehead idea" and "a terrible, terrible mistake to make." In the presidential debates leading up to the 2020 election, Biden was very hesitant and deflected the question of adding justices to the Supreme Court. In April 2021, less than three months after taking office, Biden signed Executive Order 14023 that created the Presidential Commission on the Supreme Court. This commission consisted of a group of individuals (mostly liberals) to look into reforming the highest court.

With Biden's history of being more of a mainstream Democrat, it is difficult to know whether his true beliefs coincide with the way his administration is currently governing or if he has always just been along for the ride of the Democratic Party. It is also a fair question if, at this point, he even understands what his administration is doing. Is Kamala Harris, Susan Rice, the Obamas, his wife Jill or someone else behind the decision-making? We don't know, but what we do know is that with support from much of the traditional media, the Biden Administration and radical leftists throughout the country are pushing policies and messages frighteningly similar to those in Cuba and Venezuela that led to their slide into socialism.

PART TWO

Chapter Six

In March of 2020, the world as we knew it was put on hold due to the novel virus Covid-19. Upon arrival in the United States, Covid-19 (or coronavirus) brought fear and uncertainty to the American people. We were told it had about a 6 percent death rate, and the country was temporarily locked down.

As the Covid-19 pandemic continued, most of the world figured out that we had to live with the virus rather than stop living. As the months passed, a great divide developed among the American people regarding how we should live our lives on a daily basis.

Should we send our kids to school?

Should we go to work?

Should we wear a face mask? Should others?

Should the government enforce the public wearing face masks?

Should we get together with our families for the holidays?

As the time came for children to return to school in the late summer of 2020, states and school districts set varying policies concerning how their schools would handle Covid-19. In the fall of 2020, many states such as Florida opened schools for in-person learning, while others such as California spent the semester learning through Zoom.

While in school, children are fed, able to learn and interact with their peers. Many far-left states such as California and school districts such as Los Angeles and Chicago who took so long to reopen their schools negatively affected their students and increased educational inequality in this country. These extended closures hampered the educational experience of millions of disadvantaged children, while their more privileged peers were able to continue their in- person learning experience with tutors or private schooling.

A study by Yale economist Fabrizio Zilibotti from early 2021 found that:

> "Pandemic-related school closures deepened educational inequality in the United States by severely impairing the academic progress of children from low-income neighborhoods while having no significantly detrimental effects on students from the country's richest communities."

Zilibotti also referred to a quote from American educator Horace Mann: "Education then, beyond all other devices of human origin, is the great equalizer of the conditions of men, the balance-wheel of the social machinery." The extended Covid school closures deprived children in poorer communities of this "equalizing" force.

In the fall of 2020, four children enrolled in a private school while public schools in their state were closed for in-person learning. These were the children of far-left Governor of California Gavin Newsom. Newsom confirmed this in late October of 2020, stating the following:

> "We absolutely believe that the social-emotional learning that occurs in the classroom is the best place for our kids, certainly the best place for their parents as well. And so it is absolutely incumbent to do everything in our power to provide support to our districts so that they can safely reopen."

Meanwhile, displaying the hypocrisy of the governor, the majority of the state's public school students would not be in a steady classroom setting until the fall or winter of 2021.

Small businesses suffered through the Covid lockdowns as well. In Los Angeles County there were fifteen thousand small businesses closed due to Covid, with half of them expected to be permanent closings as of early 2021. Many industries were hurt with the restaurant industry getting hit so hard that nearly a third of California's restaurants permanently closed. Newsom's own restaurant, PlumpJack Winery, was of course open throughout the majority of the pandemic.

In November of 2020, the holidays were fast approaching, and politicians around the country issued orders extending from limits on the number of people allowed in your house for a gathering to how many miles you could travel from your house, to instating curfews. States across the nation from California to Oregon, Washington, Michigan, and New York increased Covid restrictions. That same month, Governor Newsom was caught having dinner at the exclusive restaurant The French Laundry in Napa for the birthday dinner of lobbyist Jason Kinney. Also at the birthday dinner were Janus Norman, a top lobbyist for the California Medical Association and Dustin Corcoran, CEO of the California Medical Association. There were several families attending the dinner party, and masks were not being worn. This was in November of 2020—the same month that Newsom had ordered more restrictions that included almost 95 percent of Californians. Newsom apologized for the dinner, calling it a "bad mistake."

★ ★ ★

With the outbreak of Covid, Newsom issued a stay-at-home order that banned in-person church services. This order stayed in place for almost a year, and it took a ruling from the United States Supreme Court for it to be lifted. It was in place during a time in which unlimited numbers of people were allowed to be crowded together partaking in protests, many of which turned into violence and looting. In fact, Los Angeles Mayor Eric Garcetti called in the National Guard and Newsom declared a state of emergency in Los Angeles on May 30, 2020, as windows were smashed, police cars were spray-painted and set on fire, and businesses were looted in the mass chaos.

The First Amendment of the US Constitution gives us both the freedom to peacefully assemble to congregate and/or to protest. How is it constitutional or logical to deny one but allow the other? Of course, California denied the *freedom* (and the protection) in which people were peacefully assembling and allowed the one that turned to violence and chaos. It doesn't make sense, but when do today's Democrats ever make sense?!

The South Bay United Pentecostal Church in Chula Vista California took Newsom's stay-at-home order banning in-church services to the courts, asking for a temporary restraining order against the ban. In May of 2020, the US 9th Circuit Court of Appeals upheld Newsom's ban by a 2-1 decision, denying the temporary restraining order. The federal appellate judges who sided with Newsom, Jacqueline Nguyen and Barry Silverman, ruled the state's action of shuttering houses of worship due to a health emergency "does not infringe upon or restrict practices because of their religious motivation and does not in a selective manner impose burdens only on conduct motivated by religious belief."

The day after this decision by the 9th Circuit Court of Appeals, South Bay United Pentecostal Church filed an emergency motion asking the US Supreme Court to overturn the ruling. Charles LiMandri—a lawyer for the Freedom of Conscience Defense Fund who was representing the church and its bishop, Arthur Hodges III—made the following statement:

"Gov. Newsom would apparently rather litigate this case all the way to the U.S. Supreme Court than allow a single Californian to go to church. Under the governor's edicts, Bishop Hodges can bump shoulders with congregants at a shopping mall, but he can't minister to them in a safe and sanitary church sanctuary. That is blatant religious discrimination, and we hope the Supreme Court agrees."

Yes!! Thank you, Mr. LiMandri!

The US Supreme Court majority did agree. In February of 2021, they overturned the ruling of the lower court by a 6-3 vote, ending Newsom's state ban on indoor religious gatherings while allowing for capacity restrictions. Justice Neil Gorsuch, one of the six justices who voted in favor of overturning the ban, said this:

"Since the arrival of Covid-19, California has openly imposed more stringent regulations on religious institutions than on many businesses. California worries that worship brings people together for too much time. Yet, California does not limit its citizens to running in and out of other establishments; no one is barred from lingering in shopping malls, salons or bus terminals."

This government overreach shows the dangers of a *big government* and why the United States Supreme Court is so important! People need to understand why Hugo Chavez packed the Supreme Court in Venezuela and why the far left wants to pack ours. The Supreme Court should not be partisan; it should be fair and based on legal interpretation. How can any fair-minded person argue that it's ok to be shoulder to shoulder in a shopping mall or a protest but not in a church? This is simply the *state* telling you, the people, what you can and can't do! Three justices—Stephen Breyer, Elena Kagan and Sonia Sotomayor—dissented from the majority decision, continuing the unfortunate partisan rulings of many members of the Supreme Court.

★ ★ ★

It was unfortunate how divisive and political Covid became. It was often difficult to maneuver through what you saw and heard through the media—on both sides. Whether or not someone chooses to get a vaccine should be a personal choice based on data, not a political ideology. What did deserve much more media attention, however, is how the Covid vaccine was developed so quickly.

Originally coming up with the plan in April of 2020, Operation Warp Speed was officially announced by President Trump on May 15, 2020. Operation Warp Speed was a publicly funded, public-private partnership between the Trump Administration and the biomedical industry to accelerate the development, manufacturing, and distribution of Covid-19 vaccines, therapeutics and diagnostics. Several corporations worked at a rapid pace to make the vaccine available as soon as possible. It was initially funded with about $10 billion from the CARES Act and was increased to $18 billion in October of 2020. Most vaccines take years to develop, and there was originally a lot of skepticism from Democrats, including Biden and Harris. In the early fall of 2020, as Donald Trump told the United States a vaccine ready for use was imminent, Biden and Harris told Americans to be skeptical of anything the President said.

> "I would not trust Donald Trump and it would have to be a credible source of information that talks about the efficacy and the reliability of whatever he's talking about."

> —Kamala Harris, September 2020

As the world found out, just days after the November 2020 election, Donald Trump was telling the truth. On November 10, it was announced the vaccine was ready for use, and on December 11 the FDA approved emergency use authorization for a Covid vaccine by Pfizer.

The first Americans received the vaccine on December 15, 2020. The Pfizer vaccine was also the first to be fully approved by the FDA on August 23, 2021. Was the vaccine approved for use too soon? Should it have been approved at all? Do the benefits outweigh the risks?

★ ★ ★

When it was realized that Joe Biden won the presidency, it was comical how quickly the left changed their tone concerning the vaccine. It went from "We don't trust anything Trump says about this vaccine" to "Everyone needs to get this vaccine!"

So much so, in fact, that in September of 2021, the Biden Administration announced the OSHA vaccine-or-test mandate, which said it was mandatory for all US businesses employing over one hundred people to require their employees to be Covid vaccinated or undergo weekly testing. That same month, Biden issued executive orders that required federal government workers to be vaccinated. The Centers for Medicare and Medicaid Services also required vaccines for employees working in medical facilities that receive Medicaid and Medicare reimbursements—the vast majority of all healthcare workers. In addition, it was ordered that government contractors who conducted business with the federal government and all persons of all branches of the US military were to receive the Covid-19 vaccine. Over 8,400 members of the US military were discharged for not getting the Covid vaccine.

Is it logical to mandate a vaccine that doesn't even stop the transmission of the virus? Are there negative side effects associated with the vaccine that we are not aware of? Is a large employer vaccine mandate constitutional, or is it violating the right of medical freedom for persons who work for private businesses? Would it hold up in court?

★ ★ ★

In January of 2022, the Supreme Court agreed with the National Federation of Independent Businesses that the federal government's "vaccine-or-test mandate" for large employers through OSHA "exceeded its statutory authority and was therefore unlawful." This decision effectively overruled the Biden Administration's mandate, which would have affected over eighty-four million US workers. This ruling was decided by a 6-3 vote with the same three justices—Stephen Breyer, Elena Kagan and Sonia Sotomayor—dissenting.

As the final arbiter of the law, the Supreme Court is the guardian and interpreter of the Constitution. With its job to protect and interpret the Constitution, it is startling in today's Supreme Court that many of the justices don't deviate from what could be considered partisan lines in seemingly most of the court's most recognized cases.

We have recently seen how crucial the Supreme Court is in protecting the rights of Americans. In these very important decisions, they protected the First Amendment by upholding religious freedom in the country's most populous state and medical freedom for tens of millions across the nation.

Joe Biden said the following regarding the Supreme Court's large employer vaccine ruling:

> "I call on business leaders to immediately join those who have already stepped up—including one third of Fortune 100 companies—and institute vaccination requirements to protect their workers, customers, and communities."

Getting a vaccination should be a fact-based decision made by the patient with input from his or her doctor, not a government mandate! If we don't have medical freedom or control of what we put in our own bodies, what, in fact, do we have control over? If a vaccine mandate by the executive branch is enforced, what could be next? Mandatory birth control, abortions, hormonal shots…??

★ ★ ★

In the winter of 2021 to 2022, the Omicron variant of Covid-19 hit the US, and daily numbers of new cases far surpassed those of the prior year at the same time—by three, four and five times! It became common for vaccinated people to get Covid, including those who had gotten one or two boosters. It should be noted that the formulation of the flu vaccine is modified for use every year, while the Covid boosters weren't modified and ready for use for twenty-one months. The original vaccine was ready for use within seven months under the Trump Administration.

Why did it take almost two years under the Biden Administration for the formulation of the boosters to be modified? This wasn't given a thought by most people or sufficient coverage by the media. The media gave the Biden Administration a pass for the high Covid numbers while trying to place the blame on people who had not been vaccinated or more conservative politicians who didn't want to place mandates on their constituents. I guess the Democrat elites pushing this narrative wanted us to be blind to the very sketchy effectiveness of the vaccine, as well as any possible side effects from it.

The media's job is supposed to be gathering information and reporting it to the public. Unfortunately, we can no longer count on so much of the media to report accurate facts. One perfect example is the way the media vilified Governor DeSantis for his Covid approach while ignoring the facts.

Let's look at the following chart showing the number of new Covid cases around the 2021/2022 holidays.

Covid Cases

	Florida	New York	Illinois
Dec 26, 2021 (7-day avg.)	16,581	32,566	10,903
Total Cases Over 7 Days	116,067	227,962	76,321
State's Population (2020)	21.48 million	19.45 million	12.67 million
Percentage of Population	.0054	.0117	.0060

	Florida	New York	Illinois
Jan 2, 2022 (7-day avg.)	43,168	61,877	18,322
Total Cases Over 7 Days	302,176	433,139	128,254
State's Population (2020)	21.48 million	19.45 million	12.67 million
Percentage of Population	.0140	.0223	.0101

	Florida	New York	Illinois
Jan 9, 2022 (7-day avg.)	66,669	74,182	33,231
Total Cases Over 7 Days	466,683	519,274	232,617
State's Population (2020)	21.48 million	19.45 million	12.67 million
Percentage of Population	.0217	.0267	.0184

	Florida	New York	Illinois
Jan 16, 2022 (7-day avg.)	58,406	52,963	29,529
Total Cases Over 7 Days	408,842	370,741	206,703
State's Population (2020)	21.48 million	19.45 million	12.67 million
Percentage of Population	.0190	.0191	.0163

	Florida	New York	Illinois
Jan 23, 2022 (7-day avg.)	37,414	25,510	26,282
Total Cases Over 7 Days	261,898	178,570	183,974
State's Population (2020)	21.48 million	19.45 million	12.67 million
Percentage of Population	.0122	.0092	.0145

	Florida	New York	Illinois
Total Cases for Above Dates	1,555,666	1,729,686	827,869
State's Population (2020)	21.48 million	19.45 million	12.67 million
Percentage of Population that Tested Positive for All Above Dates	.0724 (7.2%)	.0889 (8.9%)	.0653 (6.6%)

Of course there are some factors to consider, such as the population density of New York City or the higher median age in Florida. (I was a bit surprised to find out that Miami actually has a higher population density than Chicago.) However, the data shows that no state or area of the country has been immune from its residents getting Covid. During the winter of 2021 to 2022, Ron DeSantis was getting slammed by the media for his Covid response, but a smaller percentage of the population had actually tested positive with Covid in his state than in the state of New York. New York, of course, had many more restrictions, such as closures, vaccine mandates and mask mandates!

In a historical context, the 1918–1919 influenza pandemic led to the deaths of an estimated 675,000 people in the United States and 50 million worldwide in those two years. Mortality rates were high in those under five years old, 20–40 years old and 65 years and older. In the United States, the influenza virus was first identified in military personnel in the spring of 1918. The population of the US in 1918–1919 was around 105 million—under one-third of what it is today. There were an estimated 830,000 deaths with Covid-19 as an attributing cause in 2020–2021.

★★★

In California, Covid further taxed and backed up an already over-worked healthcare system. Wait times to get in to see primary care physicians were already very often long, referrals are needed to see specialists (who usually have long wait times) and staffing issues became so rampant that medical procedures had to be postponed and some pharmacies had to cut hours or temporarily close!

In January of 2022, California Assembly Bill 1400 was reintro-duced from the prior year in the state legislature. Introduced by Ash Kalra, Alex Lee and Miguel Santiago of the California State Assembly, the passage of this bill would have established a single-payer health-care system for the State of California. Free healthcare always sounds appealing, but of course, it is never actually free. Assembly Bill 1400 proposed this would have been paid through **an increase in taxes— a personal income tax for anyone making more than $149,509, a payroll tax on businesses with fifty or more employees and a gross receipts tax on companies earning more than $2 million annually-**-a projected total of $163 billion annually.

For any of you who think an income of $149,509 in California is making people rich, think again! While this is a good income, it is a middle-class income. Let's look at the numbers! As of June 2022, in California, the average price for a typical home is $790,475, the aver-age monthly mortgage payment is $3,879 (calculated with the current average interest rate of 5.29 percent and 20 percent down), and the average gallon of gas is $6.37, in addition to a minimum 24 percent federal and a 9.3 percent state income tax rate.

Examples:

150K Annual Income	165K Annual Income
Monthly Income: $12,500	Monthly Income: $13,750
24% Federal Income Tax: −$3,000	32% Federal Income Tax: −$4,400

9.3% State Income Tax: −$1,163	9.3% State Income Tax: −$1,279
Insurance: −$500	Insurance: −$500
Mortgage: −$3,879	Mortgage: −$3,879
Gas: −$300	Gas: −$300
Daycare: −$1,400	Daycare: −$1,400
Food (Family of three): −$1,000	Food: −$1,000
Car payment: −$500	Car payment: −$500
Total Left: $758	Total Left: $492

It is important to note that a tax on companies based on gross receipts is before expenses. A company could earn $2 million in gross receipts, but after expenses it could have a net profit of $100,000 or less. I thought Bernie Sanders, Elizabeth Warren and those of the Progressive left wanted to fund universal healthcare through a tax on billionaires. How many Californians who make 150K a year are billionaires? How does this square? Wouldn't this have been yet another tax on the middle class?

"Free," of course, doesn't always correlate to quality. Remember, Cuba has universal healthcare. Unfortunately, healthcare in America is a problem without a solution; costs are very high, and I don't see any solution to fix it from any side. To be able to fund single-payer healthcare, taxes would increase (yes, for the middle class too), there would still be out-of-pocket expenses (just like there currently are with Medicare) and you would have to give some of your medical freedom to the government. Without it, insurance will remain unaffordable for tens of millions of Americans.

What I do know is that Californians are leaving the state in droves, and adding more taxes will only increase this outward migration!

Other estimates have a single-payer system in California costing more than $163 billion per year. The University of California Labor Center estimated the cost at $222 billion annually.

★★★

The Supreme Court drew national attention yet again in 2022 as it had its say regarding abortion as well! In June of 2022, the highest court ruled to uphold a Mississippi law that bans most abortions after fifteen weeks of pregnancy. The same day, it voted to **overturn** *Roe v. Wade*—the 1973 ruling that said abortion was a national right. Many Americans were upset about the ruling and protested across the country. As controversial and emotional as the ruling was, it was the correct decision. The job of the Supreme Court justices is to interpret the laws of the Constitution. Issues not mentioned in the Constitution are reserved for the states to decide via the Tenth Amendment. There is no mention of abortion in the Constitution; thus, it is up for each state to decide what its individual policy will be. Any national law regarding abortion would have to be passed through Congress.

"The Powers not delegated to the United States by the Constitution, nor prohibited by it to the States, are reserved to the states respectively, or to the people."

—Tenth Amendment

The privacy argument that people have attempted to make isn't valid in terms of the legality of the abortion procedure. If someone has a legal abortion, they have a right to privacy. The right to medical privacy and the legality of abortion are two separate issues.

The Supreme Court voted 6-3 to uphold the Mississippi law banning most abortions after fifteen weeks (*Dobbs v. Jackson Women's Health Organization*) and 5-4 to overturn *Roe v. Wade*. Justice John Roberts voted to uphold the Mississippi law but not to overturn *Roe v. Wade*. This is an interesting split by the Chief Justice given that by voting to uphold the Mississippi law, he voted in line with the Tenth Amendment, saying abortion legislation is up to the individual states.

The three left-leaning justices—Sotomayor, Kagan and Breyer—of course voted in favor of the progressive cause rather than the writing and obvious interpretation of the Constitution.

We shouldn't be scared of the Supreme Court making the **correct** constitutional decision. This is not a risk to democracy! What we *should* be scared of is the left wanting to *pack* the court, a preliminary draft decision being leaked (more than likely to try and intimidate members of the court) and a man caught outside Justice Kavanaugh's home with the intention of killing him!

★ ★ ★

Almost eight weeks before the Supreme Court overturned *Roe v. Wade*, an initial draft of the decision written by Justice Alito was leaked to *Politico*. This was unprecedented, as no draft decision in the modern history of the court had been disclosed publicly while a case was still pending. Chief Justice John Roberts ordered an investigation into the leak and designated the courts marshal, Gail Curley, to lead the effort.

> "To the extent this betrayal of the confidences of the Court was intended to undermine the integrity of our operations, it will not succeed. The work of the court will not be affected in any way. This was a singular and egregious breach of that trust that is an affront to the Court and the community of public servants who work here."
>
> —Chief Justice John Roberts

As of October of 2022, there was no new information regarding the source of the leak.

Quickly after the leak, protestors went to the homes of several of the Supreme Court Justices, including Brett Kavanaugh, Amy Coney Barrett and Clarence Thomas. On June 8, 2022, approximately five weeks after the draft decision was leaked and three weeks before the final decision was announced, a man was arrested outside Justice Kavanaugh's Maryland home with the intention of killing him. The man, Nicholas John Roske—twenty-six, from Simi Valley, California—was arrested about 1:50 a.m. near Kavanaugh's home.

Roske was originally spotted getting out of a cab in front of Kavanaugh's home by two deputy US marshals. After seeing the marshals standing next to their parked vehicle, Roske apparently walked down the block and called 911, telling the operator he was having suicidal thoughts and that he wanted to kill Justice Kavanaugh. Roske told authorities he "began thinking how to give his life a purpose and decided he would kill the Supreme Court justice" after finding his address on the internet. Roske had a pistol, a pistol light, ammo, a knife, duct tape, pepper spray, a screwdriver, a hammer and a crow bar upon arrest.

The protests outside of the justices' homes have been organized by radical left-wing groups, such as the extremist pro-abortion group Ruth Sent Us. As of September of 2022, Ruth Sent Us has rendezvous locations for protesters to meet before they go to the homes of Justices Kavanaugh and Roberts on Wednesdays, Clarence Thomas on Thursdays, Amy Coney Barrett on Fridays and Samuel Alito on Saturdays. They also tweeted out the name of the church Justice Barrett attends and the school her children attend, encouraging protestors to "voice your anger" by demonstrating there. Protestors also demonstrated outside the Supreme Court building in Washington, DC.

★ ★ ★

The argument that the left makes in favor of government-mandated vaccinations is contrary and hypocritical to their pro-abortion stance. I guess "My body, my choice" only applies when convenient to their narrative…

As for abortions, aside from medical reasons, "My body, my

choice" is a flawed, non-science-based argument after an unborn baby reaches a point of development where you have two bodies involved.

It is difficult to find data on the number of abortions performed per year and in which stage of the pregnancy they are performed. The numbers vary, but it appears the vast majority of abortions take place in the first trimester of the pregnancy. Based on the data I found, I would estimate between 2 and 4 percent of the abortions performed in the US per year take place after eighteen weeks of gestation. In a typical year of approximately 900,000 abortions performed annually, this would mean an estimated 18,000 to 36,000 take place after eighteen weeks.

Many states have recently made it legal to have abortions up until birth for any purpose, apparently ignoring or not caring about the advanced development of the baby. It is also difficult to find data on the reasons that abortions are performed. One 2004 survey of almost one thousand women who had abortions indicated that about 7 percent were due to health reasons of the baby or mother, less than 1 percent due to rape/incest and 86 percent were due to other reasons, such as the timing not being right, financial issues or relationship problems—other phrases for "birth control." The main argument in favor of abortion is that women should have a moral right to decide what to do with their bodies and the freedom of choice whether or not to end a pregnancy. So, according to the left, we have the right to decide what to do with our bodies when it involves taking another life, but not when it comes to what we put in our bodies?

My belief on this controversial topic is that abortions should be allowed for medical reasons where there is harm or potential harm to the mother or baby or for cases of rape/incest. For non-emergency situations there should be limits. It is sad that people who see an ultrasound at ten or eleven weeks of gestation, with the baby's limbs already moving and heart beating, still push for abortions for nonmedical reasons to take place after this point. By eighteen weeks, pain receptors are present, and by twenty-three weeks the baby can survive outside of his or her mother.

California Assembly Bill 1400 never came up for a vote in 2022, as it was realized it would fall short of the votes needed to pass.

Chapter Seven

California is one of, if not *the* most beautiful state in the nation. Its diverse landscape, picturesque coastline, majestic mountains, forests and rolling hills make it a photographer or traveler's dream. With all the natural beauty, why are so many Californians fleeing the state? Is it because of the high cost of living, the largest homelessness crisis in the nation, Covid-related closures in 2020 and 2021, or something else?

One very big reason many Californians are fleeing the state is the curriculum being instituted into its public schools. In October 2021, Governor Newsom signed California Assembly Bill 101 into law that mandated all public school students to complete a semester- long course in "ethnic studies" in order to earn a high school diploma. This ethnic studies requirement, written by State Assemblyman Jose Medina, is a blueprint of the very controversial critical race theory or (CRT). On October 8, 2021, Newsom made the following statement in regard to Assembly Bill 101:

> "I am signing Assembly Bill 101, which adds the completion of a one-semester course in ethnic studies as a public high school graduation requirement commencing with students graduating in the 2029–2030 school year.

Ethnic studies courses enable students to learn their own stories, and those of their classmates, and a number of studies have shown that these courses boost student achievement over the long run— especially among students of color.

I appreciate that the legislation provides a number of guardrails to ensure that courses will be free from bias or bigotry and appropriate for all students. The bill also expresses the Legislature's intent that courses should not include portions of the initial draft curriculum that had been rejected by the Instructional Quality Commission due to concerns related to bias, bigotry, and discrimination.

America is shaped by our shared history, much of it painful and etched with woeful injustice. Students deserve to see themselves in their studies, and they must understand our nation's full history if we expect them to one day build a more just society."

Now, let's look at the definitions of some of the required terms from the mandatory ethnic studies class:

Critical Race Theory (CRT): While manifesting differently, CRT is often engaged to offer a critical analysis of race and racism within a particular discipline, field, system of power, culture, etc. CRT draws on a collection of critical frameworks to better understand how race and racism are interwoven into the fabric of American society.

Gender: Western culture has come to view gender as a binary concept, with two rigidly fixed options—men and women. Instead of the static binary model produced through a solely physical understanding of gender, a far richer tapestry of biology, gender expression, and gender identity intersect resulting in a multidimensional array of possibilities. Thus, gender can also be recognized as a spectrum that is inclusive of various gender identities.

Whiteness: A social construct that has served as the foundation for racialization in the United States. Whiteness is the antithesis of Blackness, and is commonly associated with those that identify as white. However, Whiteness is much more than a racial identity marker, it separates those that are privileged from those that are not. Whiteness can manifest as a social, economic, political, and cultural behavior and power. For example, the "standard" or cultural "norm" are often always based on whiteness and by extension white culture, norms, and values.

People of Color: Someone who is not white. People of color as a collective identity emerged as a response to systemic racism and to assert resistance and solidarity against white supremacy. People of color are a global majority.

Hxrstory: Similar to herstory, hxrstory is used to describe history written from a more gender inclusive perspective. The "x" is used to disrupt the often rigid gender binarist approach to telling history.

These and dozens of other terms can be found on the California Department of Education's website under "Glossary and Bibliography" for the graduation-required ethnic studies class. I encourage all readers to view for themselves the divisive curriculum that the state of California is requiring their public school students to be subjected to in order to get a high school diploma.

Note that Newsom uses the phrase "free from bias or bigotry" in his statement above. Is it not bias or bigotry to divide children by their skin color?

It is also misleading and unfair given the large number of White people (including so many Conservatives and Republicans) who sacrificed so much, including their own lives, to fight for equality for all. The post-WWII American/Japanese relationship healed, and we transitioned from bitter enemies to allies within years. Why can't we heal past injustices or current divisions within the United States?

★ ★ ★

One of the steps in transforming a free country to a totalitarian one is to divide its people by wealth and by race. Anyone who has been paying attention to American politics in recent years should know the Progressive left is trying to do this in many ways, examples being dividing us into categories of liberal vs. conservative, Black vs. White, poor vs. wealthy, and even vaccinated vs. unvaccinated!

Let's look at how critical race theory is defined. Its definition from Britannica is:

> "Intellectual and social movement and loosely organized framework of legal analysis based on the premise that race is not a natural, biologically grounded feature of physically distinct subgroups of human beings but a socially constructed category that is used to oppress and exploit people of colour. Critical race theorists hold that racism is inherent in the law and legal institutions of the United States insofar as they function to create and maintain social, economic, and political inequalities between whites and nonwhites, especially African Americans."

Proponents of CRT point to racism not being an intentional prejudice, but rather a subtle one. What…? So White people are racist solely because of the color of their skin?? Now we have the double standard that if/when someone notices race, it is because they are a racist, but if they *don't* notice race, they are privileged—and thus inherently racist!? Does it not make more sense to teach history based on facts to learn from its mistakes, rather than trying to divide based on a *theory*?

Leftists and proponents of CRT use it as an answer to why there are racial disparities on issues such as poverty in the United States. Before we cover that, let's first define "theory." The first two definitions in the dictionary are as follows:

1. An idea or set of ideas that is intended to explain facts or events.
2. An idea that is suggested or presented as possibly true but that is **not known or proven to be true**.

It is true and important to know that there are racial disparities in the United States. CRT is not factual, but rather a theory to explain why these exist. Now, let's look at the facts.

Based on the rhetoric of the left, one would assume the states with the greatest income inequalities would be conservative or deep red. The chart below lists the ten states with the highest income inequality and the ten with the lowest as of 2022.

States with the Highest Income Inequality	States with the Lowest Income Inequality
1. New York	1. Alaska
2. Louisiana	2. Wyoming
3. California	3. Utah
4. Connecticut	4. New Hampshire
5. Florida	5. Hawaii
6. Massachusetts	6. Wisconsin
7. Georgia	7. Vermont
8. Texas	8. South Dakota
9. Illinois	9. Iowa
10. Mississippi	10. Nebraska

As you can see, conservative-leaning states do **not** have higher levels of income inequality. Of the ten states with the *least* overall income inequality, eight are either conservative or moderate. Those on the left claim their policies help with redistribution of wealth, which is interesting, given the wealth in conservative-leaning states is already more evenly distributed...

The following list consists of the top ten states with the most racial inequality in education and those with the least for the year 2022. This data was calculated through several metrics, such as the rate of obtaining high school diplomas and bachelor degrees and gaps in standardized testing.

States with Most Racial Inequality in Education	States with Most Racial Equality in Education
1. Wisconsin	1. Wyoming
2. Minnesota	2. West Virginia
3. Connecticut	3. New Mexico
4. New York	4. Idaho
5. Massachusetts	5. Montana
6. South Carolina	6. Oklahoma
7. Pennsylvania	7. Texas
8. Iowa	8. Arizona
9. Illinois	9. Kentucky
10. New Jersey	10. Tennessee

As you can see, the states with the most racial equality in education are overall more conservative than those with the least . The left says they are for equity, equality and helping those they like to label as minorities. So, why are Democrat-run states doing worse than conservative-leaning states regarding racial equality in education?

This chart shows the median household income by race for 2000, 2008, 2016 and 2019.

Median Household Income by Race

	Asian	White	Hispanic	Black
2000	- -	$67,920	$47,841	$45,422
2008	$78,129	$66,099	$45,129	$40,882
2016	$86,754	$69,292	$50,791	$42,684
2019	$98,174	$76,057	$56,113	$46,073

When it comes to median household income in the United States, Asians are leading other races by a significant margin. The success of Asian Americans can be traced back to education, culture and family structure, as the following charts will show. Although Hispanic families still make less than White families overall, their median incomes have increased proportionally over those of White families at every point on this chart. Black households have struggled the most, as their median household income barely increased in this nineteen-year period—just 1.4 percent.

It is difficult to believe that as of mid-2022, the current year-over-year inflation rate is over 9 percent, which is 8 percent higher than the household wages of Black Americans increased over two decades! During the tenures of the George W. Bush and Obama Administrations from 2000 to 2016, the median income for Black families actually decreased by 6 percent in sixteen years!! It is fair to point out that the median income for families of all races increased the most by far under the first three years of the Trump Administration.

Almost done with the charts, I promise! Let's look at the percentage of US adults by race over the age of twenty-five with a bachelor's degree or higher as of 2019.

Asian: 61%	Hispanic: 21%
White: 42%	Black: 28%

As Horace Mann said, "Education is the great equalizer." Babies born into a less stable family are more likely to lack success in education as compared to babies who are born into a more stable household. As a whole, those with higher levels of education go on to average higher lifetime earnings.

The following list is the percentage of babies born out of wedlock by race as of 2018:

Asian: 11.7%	Hispanic: 51.8%
White: 28.2%	Black: 69.4%

These inequalities we see in society are often tied back to the home and the culture that so many celebrities, activists, big corporations and politicians on the left support. Our society is promoting a far-left ideological culture of "It's ok, the government will take care of you," rather than successfully teaching the skills and values needed to support a family and bring prosperity to future generations.

A factor that ties in closely to racial disparities in income is the percentage of babies of that race being born in or out of wedlock. From birth, those infants born with one or zero parents in their life have a disadvantage over those born into a household with both. This is true from development in early years to emotional and behavioral stability and academic performance in school. According to a study by the National Association of Elementary School Principals, 33 percent of elementary school students from two-parent households are ranked as high achievers, as compared to only 17 percent of those from single-parent households. Those children growing up without both parents present are more likely to have emotional and behavioral problems, poor impulse control and a weaker sense of right versus wrong.

The notion that Republicans or Conservatives are the ones responsible for creating racial disparities in the United States and the Progressives are here to help is absolutely false! Let's look at Chicago. In the Windy City, almost 75 percent of Black babies are born out of wedlock (higher than the national average) and 18 percent of Black residents have a bachelor's degree or higher (lower than the national average). The last time Chicago had a non-Democratic mayor was 1931, and today, in late 2022, forty-six out of fifty members of the City Council are affiliated with the Democratic Party. The remaining four members are listed as Independent-affiliated. And yet, so many are pushing the narrative that Democrats are helping minorities.

The facts don't show that the reason for income disparity is attributed to the *theory* of CRT or systemic racism, but rather that it correlates much more closely to the breakdown of the nuclear family. The left's narrative of a White society holding down minorities obviously isn't true with Asians. Teaching children that they are inherently racist or the victims of systemic racism rather than teaching them the skills they need to succeed has not and will not help anyone. CRT is teaching our youth to pay attention to the color of their peers' skin rather than the individuals that they are. Babies are not born inherently racist!

Anyone can look up the data and see how important the nuclear family is. Has the Black Lives Matter Global Network (BLM) done this, or do they not care? One would think BLM would be trying to aid the Black nuclear family, right? BLM's "What We Believe" handout as of September 2020 said this:

> "We disrupt the Western-prescribed nuclear family structure require-
> ment by supporting each other as extended families and "villages"
> that collectively care for one another, especially our children, to the
> degree that mothers, parents and children are comfortable."

Why would they want to "disrupt" the nuclear family?

One thing we can predict is that the more nuclear families that are disrupted (of all races), the more lives will be affected—negatively!

★ ★ ★

There have been hundreds of thousands of illegal crossings at the US southern border every year for decades, and a whopping **3,817,180** documented in the first twenty full months of the Biden Administration. Why would someone leave their home and travel hundreds or thousands of miles through the oppressive heat, often paying a cartel all the money they have?

They do it for opportunity! The United States has more opportunities than their home countries do.

The United States has a plethora of millionaires, of all races. Of the approximately fifty-six million millionaires worldwide, twenty-two million of them are in the US, making the US home to 40 percent of the world's millionaires and just 4.2 percent of the world's population! Demographically, approximately 75 percent of US millionaires are White, 8 percent are Black, 8 percent are Asian and 7 percent are Hispanic. Of the approximately 332 million people in the United States in 2022, 60 percent are White, 18.5 percent are Hispanic, 13.4 percent are Black and 5.9 percent are Asian. The opportunity is there, and given the statistics on education, the number of Black millionaires in the US is actually quite impressive.

Contrary to what one may know or has been told, the majority of US millionaires—79 percent, actually—are self-made first-generation millionaires. They did not inherit their wealth! How about teaching what the possibilities and opportunities are in America, rather than what they are not...?? Rather than a mandatory ethnic studies class in California public schools, how about a mandatory class in money management...??

It needs to be asked repeatedly why those on the far left want to break down a system with opportunity, a historically large middle class and the freedoms we have. Most of them must know the failings of Cuba and Venezuela! Intellectuals have to know how quickly the US's relationship with Japan healed after the end of WWII!

Education, spending habits and investing are the most important factors in becoming a millionaire.

★ ★ ★

Now more than ever, public education is among the biggest issues for voters. We saw this in the spotlight of the 2021 election for governor of Virginia. In November of 2021, Republican candidate Glenn Youngkin defeated Democratic candidate Terry McAuliffe in a state that Donald Trump lost by ten points just a year prior. Youngkin ran on an anti-CRT platform, and although he did recommend the Covid vaccine, he was against mandating it for businesses and schools. McAuliffe wanted vaccine mandates for those over age twelve.

Glenn Youngkin also ran on the platform of providing school choice and support for every school in the state to have a police officer on-site. He criticized McAuliffe for vetoing a bill in 2017 that would have required school districts to notify parents when students are assigned reading materials considered sexually explicit, which McAuliffe called "unnecessary and potentially burdensome for educators." McAuliffe also supported changes that would have made it easier for women to get abortions in their third trimester of pregnancy.

In the months leading up to the Virginia election, a heinous incident in the state caught the attention of many voters. This was the sexual assault of a female student in the girls' bathroom by a biological male student wearing a skirt at Stone Bridge High School in Loudoun County. This May 2021 assault of the high school freshman did not receive adequate national media attention or discussion. If the assault wasn't horrible enough, the girl's father, Scott Smith, was arrested the following month at a school board meeting for getting into a verbal altercation after a woman said she didn't believe his daughter was raped. Smith was found guilty of disorderly conduct and resisting arrest two months later.

Mr. Smith, who was allegedly told by the school that the incident would be handled internally, contacted the police after the sexual assault in May of 2021. The night of Mr. Smith's arrest at the school board meeting in June, Superintendent Scott Ziegler told the school board that to his knowledge, there was no record of assaults in the restrooms. The superintendent said this in response to a question from a school board member concerning the district's transgender and gender-fluid student rights policy that allows students to use the restroom of the gender they "identify" with.

Interestingly, in August of 2021, the Loudoun County School Board voted to adopt the Virginia Department of Education's guidelines on transgender policy, which allows transgender students to compete in sports with their *preferred* gender, use the restroom and locker room of their choice and stay in rooms with those of the opposite sex on overnight trips. Many people believe this assault in the girls' bathroom three months prior was ignored or covered up by the school board and school officials who wanted the passage of the transgender policy.

So, what happened to the boy in the girls' bathroom responsible for the assault? Well, he was arrested and charged in July of 2021, then released from juvenile detention. Just three months later, he sexually assaulted another girl inside a classroom at Broad Run High School, also in Loudoun County. Later that same month, in October of 2021, the boy was convicted for the assault of Mr. Smith's daughter. Sentencing would wait until after he was due back in court for the charges of the second attack.

After the conviction, the Smith family made the following statement:

> "The sexual assault our daughter endured should never happen to any young girl, or any child, attending a public school. But because of indifference and negligence by Loudoun County Public Schools and the Loudoun School Board, it did. And now, it has happened to another girl at another Loudoun County school at the hands of the very same assailant."

In January of 2022, the boy was found guilty of abduction and sexual battery for the second incident in October of 2021. His sentencing entailed placement in a residential treatment facility and supervised probation until his eighteenth birthday, at which time he will be required to register as a sex offender. The Smiths spoke at the boy's sentencing hearing, asking that he be placed in a residential treatment center instead of juvenile hall so he would receive the help he needed and "might have a fighting chance of becoming a better human being."

Loudoun County Sheriff Michael Chapman blamed Superintendent Ziegler for the assault of the second girl. Chapman said that Ziegler was "unmistakably aware of the offense" and that he clearly knew about the May assault the day it happened, as he had sent an email to the school board advising them of the incident. This information would mean that Superintendent Ziegler was lying at the June school board meeting when he said that he wasn't aware of any sexual assaults taking place in the restrooms. The boy who committed the assault had been transferred but was allowed to stay in public schools, where a second girl was assaulted. Even with all this evidence, the Loudoun County School District has denied that there was a cover-up.

As one can imagine, this case caused an outrage among many in the community and even led to the resignation of staff. One teacher who resigned publicly made the following statement to the school board:

> "After reading about your lack of consideration for the growing population of concerned citizens in this division, clearly evidenced by this empty room tonight, where you shut the doors to the public, as well as the emails sent by the superintendent last year reminding me that a dissenting opinion is not allowed, even to be spoken in my personal life, going so far as to send a form to my colleagues and I encouraging us to fill it out if we hear one another speaking against the controversial policies being promoted by this school board and adopted in this country. Not only that, but in the last year, I was told in one of my so-called equity trainings that white

Christian able-bodied females currently have the power in our schools and that, quote, "This has to change."

Clearly you've made your point. You no longer value me or many other teachers you've employed in this county. So, since my contract outlines the power that you have over my employment in Loudoun County Public Schools, I thought it necessary to resign in front of you. School board, I quit. I quit your policies. I quit your trainings. And I quit being a cog in a machine that tells me to push highly politicized agendas on our most vulnerable constituents, the children. I will find employment elsewhere. I encourage all parents and staff in this county to flood the private schools."

★ ★ ★

On the other side of the country, the Oregon Department of Education sent information to math instructors in the state with the focus of "dismantling racism in mathematics instruction." The instructors were provided information for an online course and workbook called *A Pathway to Equitable Math Instruction* in reference to their teaching of mathematics.

How is math racist, you ask? Well, according to the eighty-two-page workbook dated May 2021, getting the right answer, showing one's work, and the idea of paternalism through the teacher providing the learning and being in charge of disseminating new information are all examples given…

According to the course workbook, white supremacy is seen in the classroom when:

There is a greater focus on getting the "right" answer than understanding concepts and reasoning.

Superficial curriculum changes are offered in place of culturally relevant pedagogy and practice.

"Good" math teaching is considered an antidote for mathematical inequity for Black, Latinx, and multilingual students.

Students are required to "show their work" in standardized, prescribed ways.

Ok. So, how is math racist again??

Maybe some people don't know or just don't care, but there are many jobs in which math is essential. Do pharmacists, doctors, engineers or contractors not need to know objective math? These are just a few of a long list of professions that use precise math on a daily basis—some to save lives! What about when dealing with our own finances? Do we not need *correct* answers here, either?

All this "woke" and absurd curriculum will do is hold back those students whose families have fewer means. Those parents with greater financial means will send their children to a different school where curriculum such as this won't be an issue. I wonder if the majority of the teachers, instructional coaches, researchers, professional development providers and curriculum writers who developed this curriculum have their children enrolled in Oregon public schools or if they, like Gavin Newsom, have found a different alternative for their own families...

The *Pathway to Equitable Math Instruction* workbook says they use California Standards for the Teaching Profession as their framework, and their website thanks the Bill and Melinda Gates Foundation "for their generous financial support of this project."

★★★

Upset parents at school board meetings who were opposed to preposterous gender policies and insane curriculum being pushed on their children drew the attention of the Biden Administration, who publicly got involved in response to an absurd and misleading letter the National School Boards Association wrote directly to the president. The letter asked for assistance from the Biden Administration in using the US Department of Justice, FBI, Department of Homeland Security and Secret Service to assess and intervene with any threats made from parents to educators or school board members. The letter continues by asking the administration to review incidents perceived as threats as domestic terrorism and hate crimes as well as asking Biden to get the Counterterrorism Division involved.

I encourage everyone to read this letter in its entirety. I have included part of it below, dated September 29, 2021, and written directly to Joe Biden from the National School Boards Association (NSBA).

> "As these acts of malice, violence and threats against public school officials have increased, the classification of these heinous actions could be the equivalent to a form of domestic terrorism and hate crimes. As such, NSBA requests a joint expedited review by the U.S. Departments of Justice, Education and Homeland Security, along with the appropriate training, coordination, investigations, and enforcement mechanisms from the FBI, including any technical assistance necessary from, and state and local coordination with, its National Security Branch and Counterterrorism Division, as well as any other federal agency with relevant jurisdictional authority and oversight. Additionally, NSBA requests that such review examine appropriate enforceable actions against these crimes and acts of violence under the Gun-Free School Zones Act, the PATRIOT Act in regards to domestic terrorism, the Matthew Shepard and James Byrd Jr. Hate Crimes Prevention Act, the Violent Interference with Federally Protected Rights statute, the Conspiracy Against Rights statute, an Executive Order to Enforce all applicable federal laws

for the protection of students and public school district personnel, and any related measure. As the threats grow and news of extremist hate organizations showing up at school board meetings is being reported, this is a critical time for a proactive approach to deal with this difficult issue."

Five days later on October 4, 2021, Attorney General Merrick Garland responded, agreeing to use the authority and resources of the federal government to "discourage, identify and prosecute these threats." The following statement is from the Attorney General's memo to the FBI and US Attorney's offices.

"The Department takes these incidents seriously and is committed to using its authority and resources to discourage these threats, identify them when they occur, and prosecute them when appropriate. In the coming days, the Department will announce a series of measures designed to address the rise in criminal conduct directed toward school personnel.

Coordination and partnership with local law enforcement is critical to implementing these measures for the benefit of our nation's nearly 14,000 public school districts. To this end, I am directing the Federal Bureau of Investigation, working with each United States Attorney, to convene meetings with federal, state, local, Tribal and territorial leaders in each federal judicial district within 30 days of the issuance of this memorandum. These meetings will facilitate the discussion of strategies for addressing threats against school administrators, board members, teachers, and staff, and will open dedicated lines of communication for threat reporting, assessment, and response."

Rightfully, there was a lot of backlash against the NSBA regarding their letter to Biden, including several State School Board Associations withdrawing from the parent organization. Less than a month later, the NSBA wrote a statement apologizing for their letter. Attorney General Garland, on the other hand, has defended his position and refused to revoke his memo even though it was supposed to be in response to the NSBA letter, which was renounced…

Very disturbingly, it appears that the NSBA had been in contact with the White House, the Department of Justice and the Department of Homeland Security before the letter was sent to Biden on September 29, 2021. There have also been reports that Biden's Education Secretary Miguel Cardona had requested the letter from the NSBA.

Five months after Merrick Garland stated that the federal government would use their powers to investigate angry parents, thirteen states signed on to a Freedom of Information Act lawsuit seeking Biden Administration records on any FBI surveillance of parents protesting school boards. Former Congressman and current Indiana Attorney General Todd Rokita is leading the lawsuit. In a quote to Fox News, Rokita said this:

> "We just want the facts. Rather than cooperate, the Biden Administration has sought to conceal and downplay its culpability. What are they hiding? Why won't they come clean? Hoosiers and all Americans deserve to know."

Given the divisive and propaganda-based subject matter being blended into public school curriculum by districts across the nation, it should be a shock to no one that angry parents are showing up at school board meetings. Could intimidation in the form of labeling or potentially prosecuting upset and angry parents as domestic terrorists aid in silencing their voices against CRT, false teachings of biological sex, vaccine mandates (potentially without parental consent), and other controversial topics?

Are you concerned about the agenda of the Biden Administration yet?

★ ★ ★

Attorney General Garland's son-in-law, Xan Tanner, is cofounder of Panorama Education, a company that has been accused by some people—including Ted Cruz on the Senate Judiciary Committee—of supporting CRT. Panorama Education's website denies being affiliated with CRT; however, visiting the website would likely make an objective person greatly doubt this. Reported from Forbes, Panorama raised $16 million in private funding in 2017, including money from the Chan Zuckerberg Initiative owned by Mark Zuckerberg and his wife, Priscilla Chan. In September 2021—the same month the NSBA letter was sent to Biden—Panorama closed on a $60 million private financing raise with venture capital firm General Atlantic. Panorama Education has contracts with the New York City Department of Education, the San Francisco Unified School District, Seattle Public Schools, the District of Columbia and the Dallas Independent School District.

The following is a statement from CEO of Panorama Education Aaron Feuer shortly after the death of George Floyd in 2020:

> "Education represents one of the most important levers for change in America. At worst, our education system can perpetuate oppression and injustice, withholding opportunity from children of marginalized communities, and allowing racism to continue unchecked. At best, our education system can combat racism, open up opportunities for children, and help every student take pride in their identity.

> We now serve 10 million students and 1,500 school districts. That puts us in a unique position to make changes to our institutions through our partnership with school districts. Important areas of impact include student voice, social-emotional learning and mental health, anti-racism practices, diversity and inclusion practices, equitable MTSS and behavior practices, conversations around race and identity, recruiting and supporting teachers of color, and systemic approaches to equity. This school year will be an especially important moment for racial equality in education, as our nation's

children begin to recover from a pandemic that has disproportionately affected Black and Brown communities and exacerbated pre-existing inequalities in American society."

The CEO of the company, with a website disclaimer saying the company does not support CRT, has the same opinionated viewpoints as what is taught in CRT. I'm sure the race, identity and equity viewpoints that Panorama wants to influence its students on are all based on science and facts... (Laughing emoji.)

★ ★ ★

Parents have the right to know what their children are learning in the classroom and what their school experiences entail. Unfortunately, political agendas, controversial curriculum, integration of the sexes in very uncomfortable situations, sexual content and even medical decisions are being pushed on our children across the country in many of the nation's public school systems—many times without the parents' knowledge.

Fortunately, there are leaders who have fought for and passed legislation in standing up for the rights of parents and students. Florida Governor Ron DeSantis and the Florida State Legislature serve as a great example. House Bill 1557, The Parental Rights in Education, was introduced in the Florida State House in January of 2022, passed by the House in February, the Senate in March, and signed by Governor DeSantis on March 28, 2022. The bill went into effect on July 1 of the same year.

This very logical piece of legislation was a tremendous win for parental and student rights by prohibiting school districts from concealing information from parents regarding their children's health, school experience or services offered by the district. Democrat politicians, the media, and many large organizations and corporations were completely dishonest about what the bill actually said and labeled it as the "Don't Say Gay" bill, a thoroughly misleading and devious title. The full text of HB1557 is only seven pages long, and I encourage everyone to read it and see for yourselves what the legislation actually says. The most important parts are as follows:

> 2. A school district may not adopt procedures or student support forms that prohibit school district personnel from notifying a parent about his or her student's mental, emotional, or physical health or well-being, or a change in related services or monitoring, or that encourage or have the effect of encouraging a student to withhold from a parent such information. School district personnel may not discourage or prohibit parental notification of and involvement in critical decisions affecting a student's mental, emotional, or physical health or well- being. This subparagraph does not prohibit a school district from adopting procedures that permit school personnel to withhold such information from a parent if a reasonably prudent person would believe that disclosure would result in abuse, abandonment, or neglect, as those terms are defined [...].

> 3. Classroom instruction by school personnel or third parties on sexual orientation or gender identity may not occur in kindergarten through grade 3 or in a manner that is not age-appropriate or developmentally appropriate for students in accordance with state standards. [...]

> 5. At the beginning of the school year, each school district shall notify parents of each healthcare service offered at their student's school and the option to withhold consent or decline any specific service. Parental consent to a health care service does not waive the parent's right to access his or her student's educational or health records or to be notified about a change in his or her student's services or monitoring as provided by this paragraph.

> 6. Before administering a student well-being questionnaire or health screening form to a student in kindergarten through grade 3, the school district must provide the questionnaire or health screening form to the parent and obtain the permission of the parent.

The following are statements from Governor DeSantis and Lieutenant Governor Jeanette Nunez regarding HB1557:

"Parents' rights have been increasingly under assault around the nation, but in Florida we stand up for the rights of parents and the fundamental role they play in the education of their children. Parents have every right to be informed about services offered to their child at school, and should be protected from schools using classroom instruction to sexualize their kids as young as five years old." –Governor DeSantis

"Parental Rights in Education empowers Florida's parents and safeguards our children. This bill refuses to allow school boards and teachers unions the ability to hide information about students from their parents. In addition, it prohibits classroom discussion in grades K-3 on gender orientation and sexual identity. Throughout this legislative session, this bill has been maliciously maligned by those who prefer slogans and sound bites over substance and common sense. Fortunately, Governor DeSantis and I believe that parents should have a say. We will not back down to woke corporations and their same tired tactics that are steeped in hypocrisy. As a mother of three, I am committed to protecting the rights of parents." –Lieutenant Governor Jeanette Nunez

This is the statement from White House Press Secretary Karine Jean-Pierre the day Florida's Parental Rights in Education went into effect:

"Today, some of Florida's most vulnerable students and families are more fearful and less free. As the state's shameful "Don't Say Gay" law takes effect, state officials who claim to champion liberty are limiting the freedom of their fellow Americans simply to be themselves. Already, there have been reports that "Safe Space" stickers are being taken down from classrooms. Teachers are being instructed not to wear rainbow clothing. LGBTQI+ teachers are being told to take down family photos of their husbands and wives—cherished family photos like the ones on my own desk."

House Bill 1557 does **not** discriminate against anyone. It simply ensures parental rights and says there cannot be classroom instruction on sexual orientation or gender identity in kindergarten through third grade—both completely logical policies. It also refers to sexual orientation or gender identity as a whole, not just specific ones pertaining to the LGTBQ community. The problem is that most people get their information from the media—the media that spins (or omits) the truth!

If teachers were forced to take down family photos, it would be due to an individual school district policy, not HB 1557. There was confusion over the bill at first, but it appears the press secretary's statement is more propaganda from the Biden Administration!

★ ★ ★

We need to speak out and be involved where we can have an influence. We can do this by attending school board meetings, communicating with teachers, school staff and our children. Be aware of the courses and subject matter being taught to your children by looking at course syllabuses, going to school district websites or state department of education websites. Always talk to your children! Also, make sure you vote! Vote not only in national elections, but also in state and local ones where positions such as mayors, judges, district attorneys, and school board members are decided.

Over the next several years, we will see more and more parents enrolling their children in private schools. Many families will pack up and move to a new school district or state where their child(ren) can get a good education and have a positive school experience without being subjected to agendas or radical-left political ideology.

Governor Ron DeSantis

Ron DeSantis got his undergraduate degree from Yale and his law degree from Harvard, graduating with honors from both. He earned his commission in the US Navy as a JAG officer and later was deployed to Iraq as an advisor to a US Navy Seal Commander. As a US congressional representative from 2013 to 2018, DeSantis fought for term limits, sponsored legislation to make it easier for the military to prosecute sexual assault, and even refused his congressional pension and health care plan, as he is opposed to special deals for politicians! Before getting elected to Congress, he also served as a federal prosecutor, where he targeted and convicted child predators.

The city of Chicago is divided into fifty legislative districts or wards. Each district is represented by an alderman who is elected by their constituency to serve a four-year term. The fifty aldermen comprise the Chicago City Council, which serves as the legislative branch of government of the city of Chicago.

The top five large US cities with the greatest income inequality as of 2019 are Atlanta, Miami, New Orleans, New York City and Cleveland.

Over the last decade, the gap between women and men attending and graduating from college has widened. In a trend that began in the early 1980s and has continued to increase, women now make up over 59 percent of those enrolled in post-secondary education. Total enrollment rates have been declining since 2012, when 11.6 million women and 8.6 million men were enrolled. New college applicants for 2021 to 2022 totaled 3,805,978 women and 2,815,810 men. Assuming this trend continues, two women will earn a college degree for every man within the next few years. Poor and working-class White men are enrolling at the lowest rates. There are many factors that this trend can be attributed to but it's worth the debate that men (in particular White men) who haven't even started their careers don't want to be subjected to the "woke" and propaganda-filled agenda so many colleges and universities across the nation have adopted.

I was not able to find any statements made by either Joe Biden or Kamala Harris regarding these sexual assaults in Loudoun County, Virginia. For such a controversial subject and heinous incident, it received an inadequate amount of national media attention.

Chapter Eight

In *The Communist Manifesto*, Karl Marx wrote about revolutionizing the mode of production and creating a new social order. Here are the first six of his objectives in creating a Communist society:

1. Abolition of property in land and application of all rents of land to public purposes.
2. A heavy progressive or graduated income tax.
3. Abolition of all right of inheritance.
4. Confiscation of the property of all emigrants and rebels.
5. Centralisation of credit in the hands of the State, by means of a national bank with State capital and an exclusive monopoly.
6. Centralisation of the means of communication and transport in the hands of the State.

The radical left in America has unfortunately closed in on accomplishing some of Karl Marx's goals. Just as they once did in Cuba and Venezuela, some far-left policies sound good at first—but the more the government takes control, raises taxes, and takes away freedoms, the more residents flee! We are currently witnessing a huge domestic migration of people from blue states such as California, Illinois and New York to traditionally red states such as Texas, Florida, Georgia and Arizona. The problem is that the residents fleeing the blue states often take their destructive voting habits with them. You would think they would learn, but many of them don't!

The more taxes we pay and the more money we spend on essential goods and services, the less money we have. The less money we have, the less independence we have. Our property, bank accounts and investments are all of the financial assets most of us have, and even those are being greatly threatened by the Progressive left.

★ ★ ★

In September of 2021, Biden nominated Säule Omarova to be Comptroller of the Currency, a position in charge of regulating the nation's banks. If her nomination had been approved, she would have been responsible for regulating the assets of over one thousand banks. Omarova, who grew up in the former Soviet Union, seems to have brought the Communist ideas of her former country with her to the States. In October of 2020, she wrote a paper called "The People's Ledger," saying this:

> "It offers a blueprint for a comprehensive restructuring of the central bank balance as the basis for redesigning the core architecture of modern finance. Focusing on the U.S. Federal Reserve System (the Fed), the Article outlines a series of structural reforms that would radically redefine the role of a central bank as the ultimate public platform for generating, modulating, and allocating financial resources in a democratic economy—the People's Ledger."

Justifiably, Biden's nomination of Omarova caused much controversy and fear. Her ideas would change the banking system so that the deposit accounts of all Americans would be handled by the Federal Reserve (note the word "allocating"), replacing private bank accounts and creating a banking monopoly by the federal government on all banking deposits! Capitalism guarantees the right to private property. A main tenet of Communism is that all property is controlled by the central government. Which form of government does it sound like Omarova supports??

Joe Biden likes to refer to himself as a traditional Democrat even though throughout his presidential campaign and from day one of his presidency, his administration has constantly and consistently governed and catered to the far left. This has been done in all facets, including with his nominations for cabinet positions. Those on the Progressive left were thrilled with Omarova's nomination, as socialist Senator Elizabeth Warren of Massachusetts said, "Säule Omarova's nomination to lead the OCC is tremendous news. Säule is an excellent choice to oversee and regulate the activities of our nation's largest banks, and I have no doubt she'll be a fearless champion for consumers."

Here is a September 23, 2021, statement from the White House listed under Omarova's name as nominee for Comptroller of the Currency: "If confirmed, Omarova will be the first woman and person of color to serve as Comptroller."

Ok, Biden Administration, can you PLEASE stop virtue signaling, hire the BEST person for the job and work on IMPROVING the country! Since this administration has taken over, the United States has suffered from major problems, such as soaring inflation, major issues with the supply chain, illegal immigration, foreign policy disasters and continued high crime! These issues were either created or worsened by the incompetence of the executive branch starting after Biden was inaugurated. Meanwhile, the administration continues to pander to those virtue signalers on the far left and either ignore or deflect blame on every problem the country is facing! Rather than trying to be politically correct and virtue signal, how about trying to solve problems?!

★ ★ ★

In order for presidential nominations to be confirmed, they have to pass by a majority vote in the Senate. The Republicans in the Senate Confirmation Hearing were critical of Omarova's Communist ideas. During the Senate hearing, Republican Senator Pat Toomey from Pennsylvania said this:

> "My concern with Prof. Omarova is her long history of promoting ideas that she herself describes as "radical." I agree that they are radical. But I'd also describe them as socialist. In fact, I've never seen a more radical nominee to be a federal regulator."

> Let's talk about some of Prof. Omarova's radical ideas. For starters, she wants to "effectively end banking as we know it." What does that mean? Well, she's told us.

> In "The People's Ledger," a paper she published just last month, she outlined her plan for nationalizing retail banking. Under her plan, "central bank accounts fully replace—rather than uneasily co-exist with—private bank deposits."

> In other words, you couldn't have an account with your local community bank. Your money would be held by the government at the Federal Reserve.

> Countless Americans were outraged over recent Democrat plans for the IRS to get their personal bank account information. Imagine their reaction to the government actually taking over their bank accounts.

> Prof. Omarova also has a proposal to control the money supply through these individual FedAccounts, including when necessary "implementing a contractionary monetary policy by debiting" those accounts. For those of us who are not accountants, debiting means subtracting.

> This, she allows, could be "perceived as the government 'taking away' people's money." I think I know why—because it is the government taking away people's money.

Prof. Omarova's plan would devastate all banks, but especially community ones that rely on deposit-taking for lending money to local businesses and residents.

Taken in their totality, her ideas amount to a socialist manifesto for American financial services.

These are exactly the kind of socialist ideas that have failed everywhere in the world they've been tried."

Fortunately, in addition to their Republican counterparts, five Democratic Senators said they would not approve Omarova's nomination, and she withdrew from consideration for the position. The five Democratic Senators who opposed the Biden nomination of Omarova were: Kyrsten Sinema and Mark Kelly of Arizona, John Hickenlooper of Colorado, Jon Tester of Montana and Mark Warner of Virginia. Knowing this, anyone who votes for Biden or any of the other forty-five Democratic Senators who did not object to Omarova's nomination is voting for a candidate who supports or at least does not object to Communism. The Progressive left, including President Biden, were upset the nomination failed and accused the Republican Senators of personal attacks toward Omarova, apparently forgetting about their own attacks on Brett Kavanaugh during his confirmation hearing just three years earlier.

Upon withdrawing herself from consideration, Omarova made the following statement: "I deeply value President Biden's trust in my abilities and remain firmly committed to the Administration's vision of a prosperous, inclusive, and just future for our country."

Just like Fidel Castro and Hugo Chavez, Communists like to make promises using words such as "inclusive," "just," "free" and "equitable" to gain support. Once they gain power, however, the large central government becomes totalitarian—leading to empty shelves, mass poverty and loss of freedoms for those to whom they falsely promised a better life!

★ ★ ★

A federal government that becomes too big and too partisan is incredibly dangerous! The United States federal government has reached this point. Departments of the federal government have used their power to investigate and intimidate those with more moderate or traditional viewpoints while they fail to investigate cases that might hurt the Progressive cause.

We have already talked about the Biden Department of Justice threatening to label upset parents as domestic terrorists. What about the prosecution of January 6th rioters vs. BLM and Antifa rioters? The Biden DOJ quickly dismissed the charges against a very large percentage of rioters charged with federal crimes in Portland, including felonies such as assaulting a federal officer. Meanwhile, the FBI has been tracking down and pursuing prosecution for any capitol rioter charged with violence as well as many charged with trespassing. How about Hunter Biden? What about the *Roe v. Wade* draft leak? This is a potential threat to democracy, right? Why is the FBI not investigating the source of the leak? Does the Biden DOJ try to avoid getting involved in cases that could hurt the Democratic Party?

★ ★ ★

Another department of the federal government that Americans need to be cognizant of is the Department of the Treasury, specifically the IRS. Having been introduced and passed in the House in the fall of 2021, H.R. 5376 passed the Senate in August of 2022 by a 51-50 vote and was signed into law that same month by the president. This bill, deceivingly called the Inflation Reduction Act of 2022, approves around $80 billion in funding for the IRS over the next nine years. Included in this is over $45 billion strictly for determination of and enforcement of owed taxes. Don't believe me? The following is straight from H.R. 5376:

Part 3—Funding the Internal Revenue Service and Improving Taxpayer Compliance

SEC. 10301. ENHANCEMENT OF INTERNAL REVENUE SERVICE RESOURCES.

IN GENERAL.—The following sums are appropriated, out of any money in the Treasury not otherwise appropriated, for the fiscal year ending September 30, 2022:

(1) INTERNAL REVENUE SERVICE.—

    (A) GENERAL.—

        (i) TAXPAYER SERVICES.—For necessary expenses of the Internal Revenue Service to provide taxpayer services, including pre-filing assistance and education, filing and account services, taxpayer advocacy services, and other services as authorized by 5 U.S.C. 3109, at such rates as may be determined by the Commissioner, $3,181,500,000 to remain available until September 30, 2031: Provided, That these amounts shall be in addition to amounts otherwise available for such purposes.

        (ii) ENFORCEMENT.—For necessary expenses for tax enforcement activities of the Internal Revenue Service to determine and collect owed taxes, to provide legal and litigation support, to conduct criminal investigations (including investigative technology), to provide digital asset monitoring and compliance activities, to enforce criminal statutes related to violations of internal revenue laws and other financial crimes, to purchase and hire passenger motor vehicles (31 U.S.C. 1343 (b)), and to provide other services as authorized by 5 U.S.C. 3109, at such rates as many be determined by the Commissioner, $45,637,400,000, to remain available until September 30, 2031: Provided, That these amounts shall be in addition to amounts otherwise available for such purposes.

        (iii) OPERATIONS SUPPORT.—For necessary expenses of the Internal Revenue Service to support taxpayer services and enforcement programs, including rent payments; facilities services; printing; postage; physical security; headquarters and other IRS- wide administration activities; research and statistics of income; telecommunications; information technology development, enhancement, operations, maintenance, and security; the hire of passenger motor vehicles (31 U.S.C. 1343 (b)); the operations of the Internal Revenue Service Oversight Board; and other services as authorized by 5 U.S.C. 3109, at such rates as may be determined by the Commissioner, $25,326,400,000, to remain available until September 30, 2031: Provided, That these amounts shall be in addition to amounts otherwise available for such purposes.

What does this mean? Well, the Internal Revenue Service is going to receive an additional $70 billion over the next nine years for purposes such as investigating tax returns, performing audits and collecting any taxes that they determine are owed. And this is, ironically, paid for with taxpayer dollars! The statement from the White House says that H.R. 5376 is supposed to create $124 billion in savings over ten years from generating taxes already owed by wealthy people and large corporations.

The FBI is a part of the Department of Justice. They answer to the Attorney General.

Not one Republican senator voted for H.R. 5376. Kamala Harris broke the 50-50 tie in the Senate, showing once again the importance of those Georgia runoff elections in January of 2021.

The IRS is a bureau of the Department of the Treasury.

Who do the Progressives consider to be wealthy? They will tell you they want to fund universal healthcare by taxing billionaires and large corporations, but lawmakers in California proposed to fund universal healthcare in their state by increasing taxes for those making over $149,000 per year and businesses making over $2 million annually in gross profits. Then you look at the number of billionaires in the US, which was reportedly 724 as of 2022. However, a report from the Treasury Department says that the additional funding will allow the IRS to hire roughly an additional 87,000 employees, including at least 5,000 new enforcement personnel! The numbers don't square up, and the federal government just keeps getting larger and larger...

★ ★ ★

The Supreme Court was established in 1789 after the Judiciary Act of 1789 was approved by Congress and signed into law by President George Washington. It first assembled in February of 1790. The Supreme Court is the most powerful body in the United States, as the Constitution grants it ultimate jurisdiction over all laws. As the final arbiter of the law, the Court is charged with ensuring the American people the promise of equal justice under law and thereby also functions as guardian and interpreter of the Constitution. The Supreme Court originally consisted of six justices, and there have been nine since 1869. The president has the power to nominate the justices and the nominees must be passed through the Senate by majority vote.

In 1983, as a senator, Joe Biden called President Franklin Roosevelt's 1937 plan to pack the Supreme Court a "bonehead idea." In October of 2019, on the campaign trail seeking the Democratic nomination for president, Biden said: "We add three justices. Next time around, we lose control, they add three justices. We begin to lose any credibility the court has at all."

In the months leading up to the 2020 presidential election, Biden kept deflecting the question of court-packing but did say he "was not a fan of court-packing" in October—just weeks before the election.

In April 2021, less than three months after his inauguration, Biden signed an executive order creating the Presidential Commission on the Supreme Court of the United States. The commission's purpose was to provide an analysis of the principal arguments in the contemporary public debate for and against Supreme Court Reform. That same month, Democrats in the Senate and the House introduced legislation to pack the court by adding four justices. It requires just a majority vote in both houses of Congress and the president's approval to add justices to the Supreme Court. Fortunately, at least two Democratic senators disapproved, and it never came to a vote in Congress!

The job of the Supreme Court is to interpret the law and make rulings based on the Constitution. It should not be partisan! It is already very concerning that the justices are labeled as conservative or liberal and so often rule in parallel to that philosophy. Packing the Supreme Court would remove checks and balances from our government, serving as a giant step in the direction of totalitarianism! You read how quickly Hugo Chavez packed the highest court in Venezuela and what has happened under that regime. If the Democrats had succeeded in adding justices to the highest court, we could have counted on a series of partisan majority rulings in favor of strong central government powers, such as closure of churches, vaccine mandates and overhauls in criminal justice, education and finance, leading straight to socialism.

The Supreme Court is the most powerful body in the United States, but the people still have the power. We hold this power by our right to vote! Remember, the president nominates the Supreme Court justices, and they are approved by majority vote in the senate. All elections are important, and they all matter!

The Presidential Commission on the Supreme Court of the United States came up with a 294 page Draft Final Report in December 2021. It said nothing of significance.

Chapter Nine

In the months leading up to the 2020 general election, it was impossible for any cognizant person to completely avoid politics. Whether the topic was Covid-19, the presidency of Donald Trump, or rioters burning and looting American cities, it was impossible to get on your device and avoid all the chaos. Many of these factors led to the highest voter turnout in US election history, with over 155 million ballots cast for the presidential ticket. Joe Biden won the popular vote by around 7 million total votes, but it was razor-thin in the Electoral College, with approximately 43,000 votes between the states of Arizona, Georgia and Wisconsin that decided the election. Nevada, North Carolina, and Pennsylvania also had extremely narrow voter margins.

In addition to having tight margins, the 2020 presidential election became the most controversial in US history. The fact that Donald Trump had an early lead on election night that was lost through the high volume of mail-in ballots tabulated over the following days led to public suspicion and distrust as well as continuous accusations of voter fraud from the 45th President.

Biden benefitted from unfair and bended mainstream media coverage in addition to enormous financial contributions, the latter of which likely helped register and increase turnout for likely Democrat voters. The 2020 election undoubtedly had issues that need to be fixed, but the stats show that there was not widespread fraud in terms of phony votes.

Two major issues with the 2020 election were the length of time it took to count and/or tabulate the ballots and the outside ballot drop boxes. All votes need to be in by election night and, with few exceptions, they should be counted and tabulated within twenty-four hours of the polls closing. The data shows that registered voters--not dead people, illegal immigrants, or fake voters were the ones who voted, but the states need to improve their voting systems to avoid future election chaos.

One thing we should all agree on is that there have to be fair elections. There has to be easy opportunity to vote, security of votes and timely counting and tabulating of ballots. A form of identification would help with voter security. It should be required for anyone voting by a mail-in ballot to write their Social Security number, driver's license number, or state ID number for verification in addition to the signature. If a state(s) decides to provide all registered voters a voter ID card, the voters in that state would logically use that as identification. With today's technology, facial recognition software could also be a viable option for some voters not able to make it to the polls. The voter should still be required to sign their ballot, but signatures should not be disqualified unless the aforementioned identification also doesn't match. Filling out a mail-in ballot and taking it into the precinct to place in the ballot box with the above criteria should be permitted. It should also be permitted to take one ballot for a family member who is a registered voter and follows the above identification criteria if that person can't make it to the polls due to an extenuating circumstance. The form of identification, whether it be a voter ID card or a state ID, should be available at no cost to voters.

The outside ballot drop boxes are a different story. We can only speculate how many people filled out ballots for multiple friends or family members and dropped several in one of the outside boxes. We also heard of instances such as a drop box catching fire or mail-in ballots being tampered with. It makes a lot more sense to have the ballot boxes inside the voting precinct to restrict potential tampering and increase voter confidence. Voters would be able to drop off their ballots during precinct hours.

★ ★ ★

It is possible that mail-in-ballots in Clark County (Nevada), Maricopa County (Arizona), or Fulton County (Georgia) had a significant enough impact to flip those states, but the numbers show that the suburbs and traditional battleground counties decided the 2020 election, not phony or even regular votes in inner cities.

In the moderately populated Pennsylvania counties of Erie, Lackawanna, Monroe, Northampton, Lehigh and Dauphin, Joe Biden gained a combined 35,878 net votes in 2020 over Hillary Clinton's margin in the 2016 election. These counties are home to mid-sized cities such as Erie, Scranton, Allentown, and the state capital, Harrisburg. In the four counties of Chester, Delaware, Montgomery and Bucks—which are considered the suburban Philadelphia area—Trump lost a combined net 104,741 votes from the 2016 election to the 2020 election. In Philadelphia, which is its own county, Trump actually **gained a net 3,957 votes** in his re-election bid.

Pennsylvania (Mid-Sized Non-Suburban Cities)

County	Year	Trump Total Votes	Clinton/Biden Total Votes
Erie	2016	60,069	58,112
	2020	66,869	68,286
Dauphin	2016	60,683	64,706
	2020	66,408	78,983

Lackawanna	2016	48,384	51,983
	2020	52,334	61,991
Monroe	2016	33,386	33,918
	2020	38,726	44,060
Northhampton	2016	71,736	66,272
	2020	83,854	85,087
Lehigh	2016	73,690	81,324
	2020	84,259	98,288
Total (Above Counties)	2016	347,948	356,315
	2020	392,450	436,695

Pennsylvania (Philadelphia Suburbs)

County	Year	Trump Total Votes	Clinton/Biden Total Votes
Chester	2016	116,114	141,682
	2020	128,565	182,372
Delaware	2016	110,667	177,402
	2020	118,532	206,423
Montgomery	2016	162,731	256,082
	2020	185,460	319,511
Bucks	2016	164,361	167,060
	2020	187,367	204,712
Total (Above Counties)	2016	553,873	742,226
	2020	619,924	913,018

Philadelphia

Year	Trump Total Votes	Clinton/Biden Total Votes
2016	108,748	584,025
2020	132,470	603,790

In his 2020 re-election bid in the state of Wisconsin, Trump lost a combined net 19,347 votes in the five counties of Brown, La Crosse, Eau Claire, Ozaukee and Waukesha. He lost the state of Wisconsin by just 20,682 votes. I could have easily added another chart showing the votes in Wisconsin, but I didn't want to bore you too badly. :)

Across the nation, 2020 was a higher turnout election than 2016—in rural, urban and suburban America. The conservative and more rural areas ran up the Republican vote more than big cities ran up the Democrat vote. As just one example, the southern (and conservative) Pennsylvania counties of Somerset, Bedford and Fulton had a combined voter turnout of 82 percent in the 2020 presidential election, up from 71 percent in 2016. Philadelphia County had a 66 percent voter turnout in 2020, up from 62 percent four years prior. In addition, from 2016 to 2020, Donald Trump's vote percentage in Philadelphia County actually improved by over 2 percent. This was not an anomaly, as Trump received higher vote shares in several of the nation's largest cities in 2020, including the three most populous in the country: New York City, Los Angeles and Chicago! He also improved in Miami, Las Vegas and Detroit while receiving virtually the same vote shares in Milwaukee and Houston. The suburban and swing counties that often decide state and nationwide elections did so in the 2020 presidential election.

Population shifts also need to be taken into account. We have been seeing a migration of northerners from Democrat-run metropolitan areas, such as Chicago, Detroit, Philadelphia and New York, to traditionally conservative states. Many Californians are also fleeing to new states, hoping for greener pastures. The problem is that these new residents often bring their destructive voting habits with them to their new state. You would think they would vote against the policies that brought high crime, taxes and regulations in their former states…

Traditionally blue or moderate Midwestern states from recent decades, such as Iowa, Wisconsin, Michigan, Ohio, and Pennsylvania, are trending more red, while traditionally red states like Arizona, Texas and Georgia are trending the opposite direction. These trends were key factors in the outcomes of both the 2016 and 2020 elections.

Did President Trump look at data from the individual counties, cross-reference votes to registered voters, or consider voting trends from prior elections before he made accusations of voter fraud? Trump continuously said the election was "fraudulent," "rigged," "stolen," "rigged via Dominion voting machines" as well as saying Mike Pence needed to veto the certification of the states on January 6, 2021. He also said on multiple occasions that he "won the election in a landslide." The facts, however, indicate otherwise, and Mr. Trump's repeated accusations of a stolen election led to more chaos in the country and, in the eyes of many, smeared his accomplishments as president.

Understanding the great danger of the Progressive left, it was frustrating to watch the way Donald Trump handled the aftermath of the 2020 election. He needs to follow the facts and make realistic arguments based on them. Some election processes need to be fixed but Donald Trump's actions did not help the Republican Party or the country as a whole. The post-election chaos, specifically surrounding Georgia, likely cost Republican Senators David Perdue and Kelly Loeffler their seats in the Georgia runoff election, in turn costing Republicans their majority in the Senate.

Although many people refuse to listen to or acknowledge this, it isn't in the best interest of the Republican Party, Conservatives, or the country as a whole for Donald Trump to run for president again. This is due to personality, not policy. His policies, particularly his economic and foreign policies, were very effective. He did not govern in a divisive way, and Americans of all races financially prospered more while he was in office than they had under the Obama or Bush Administrations. The issue many voters have with him is his chaos.

His attempts to change the election results in Georgia—along with his failures of not being able to *talk less* or, as Bill Barr said, his "pettiness"—make a candidate who can stay focused on the facts, fight the Progressive left on policy and unite more voters a preferable choice in 2024. There are plenty of accomplishments from his presidency that Donald Trump can boast about. Why doesn't he focus more on the positives, such as the median income statistics from my chart earlier? I don't know if the former president is delusional, just can't accept defeat or genuinely believes that he did win the election in a landslide, but his message and inadequate factual presentation regarding the 2020 election are not winning him over voters.

A new face would be a sight for sore eyes on the Republican ballot in 2024. If we lose our democracy in America, it won't be because Donald Trump gets elected again and becomes a dictator, but rather because the hatred for him brings a rise of power to the far left.

In Georgia, a candidate needs to receive at least 50 percent of the total vote to avoid a runoff election. In the 2020 general election, David Perdue had 49.7 percent of the vote and his Democratic challenger had 47.9 percent, with a third candidate getting 2.3 percent. In the runoff election two months later, the Democratic challenger defeated Perdue 50.6 percent to 49.4 percent. Kelly Loeffler also lost to the Democratic challenger she was facing in the special election on January 5, 2021.

★★★

I'm sure most of the country never thought about Georgia's elections until after election night in November of 2020. There were, however, many in the Georgia state legislature and government offices who were aware of problems and made attempts to fix them long before the 2020 general election.

The 2018 Georgia election brought a state record turnout for a midterm election and, with it, long lines and wait times. In February of 2020, Georgia Republican State Senators Kennedy, Dugan, Gooch, Jones and Mullis drafted Senate Bill 463, designed to reduce wait times and other issues at the voting precincts. The bill would have required election officials to make the necessary changes for smoother elections with shorter wait times. The following was the main objective of SB 463:

> If, at the previous primary, election, or runoff, a precinct contained more than 2,000 electors and if electors desiring to vote on the day of a primary, election, or runoff had to wait in line more than one hour before checking in to vote, the superintendent shall either reduce the size of said precinct so that it shall contain not more than 2,000 electors in accordance with the procedures prescribed by this chapter for the division, alteration, and consolidation of precincts no later than 60 days before the next general election or provide additional voting equipment or poll workers or both before the next general election. For administering this Code section, the chief manager of a precinct shall submit a report thereof, under oath, to the superintendent of the reported time from an elector entering the line to checking in to vote. Such wait time shall be measured no fewer than three different times throughout the day including morning, midday, and prior to the close of the polls or as otherwise designated by the election superintendent or the Secretary of State, and such results shall be recorded on a form provided by the Secretary of State. Any such change in the boundaries of a precinct

shall conform with the requirements of subsection (a) [...]. [Note: Subsection a is the 2,000 voters per precinct requirement.]

One would think anyone, regardless of political affiliation, could agree on shorter lines at voting precincts, right? Wrong! Senate Bill 463 was strongly opposed by Democrats and voting rights groups. The main reason given was that it would be *confusing* to voters.

Ok... Voters get notified of their precinct location weeks before the election, and county election offices or the secretary of state can confirm this location or answer any questions voters may have. Contact information for the county election offices can be found at ease, and you can easily call and speak with a live person. It is very important to note that precinct locations do sometimes change. My voting location has changed before and there is a decent chance yours has too...

Lauren Groh-Wargo, the CEO of the voting rights group Fair Fight Action founded by Stacey Abrams, made this statement: "They're going to sow a lot of confusion here. This bill is creating additional barriers to voting."

What?? How would shorter lines increase barriers to voting? Confusing?? How is this confusing? What an insult to voters' intelligence. Voters receive their precinct location by mail and can easily call or look up their location online. Can Democrats be any more dishonest or insulting to their voting base?

> "The real oddity is that the complaint we've heard before is that folks have to drive too far or precincts aren't readily available. You've now made precincts closer to where people live. I don't see how that's not a good thing."
>
> —Georgia State Senator Kennedy, One of the Bill's Sponsors

Senate Bill 463 was approved in the Georgia State Senate 35-19 along party lines, with not one Democrat voting for it. Next, the bill went to the State House of Representatives where it was held up, never reaching a vote. It was withdrawn in the Georgia State House on June 25, 2020.

In early October of 2020, the Georgia Secretary of State's (SOS) office told four counties—Fulton, DeKalb and Gwinnett in the Atlanta metro area and Chatham County in southeast Georgia—to avoid the problems of long lines, late opening and closing of polls, and absentee ballot issues that had occurred there in the primaries. The SOS asked for weekly updates on poll worker training, polling places and line management plans. The office of the Georgia Secretary of State, led by Brad Raffensperger (a Republican), had endorsed Senate Bill 463.

Anyone who believes in honesty and objectivity should want to correct any problems in the voting precincts and have a smooth election, right? Well, Republicans in the state of Georgia did. They tried to be proactive and fix potential problems before the election, only to run into opposition from the Democrats! The presidential race in the state of Georgia was not called until November 13, 2020—ten full days after Election Day.

★ ★ ★

Senate Bill 202 (SB 202) was introduced on February 17, 2021. It was quickly passed in the Georgia House and Senate, then signed into law by Governor Brian Kemp on March 25, 2021. The same as what was intended with SB 463, SB 202 was designed to help avoid future election problems by *shortening* lines at the polls, *expanding* voting hours to require two mandatory Saturday voting days, requiring votes to be counted and tabulated in a timely manner, prohibiting people from giving away food and drinks to voters waiting in lines and shortening the time from the general election to the potential runoff. The following is direct text and many of the most important parts of SB 202:

SECTION 18. [...]

(b) If, at the previous general election, a precinct contained more than 2,000 electors and if electors desiring to vote on the day of the election had to wait in line more than one hour before checking in to vote, the superintendent shall either reduce the size of such precinct so that it shall contain not more than 2,000 electors in accordance with the procedures prescribed by this chapter for the division, alteration, and consolidation of precincts no later than 60 days before the next general election or provide additional voting equipment or poll workers, or both, before the next general election. For administering this Code section, the chief manager of a precinct which contained more than 2,000 electors at the previous general election shall submit a report thereof to the superintendent of the reported time from entering the line to checking in to vote. Such wait time shall be measured no fewer than three different times throughout the day (in the morning, at midday, and prior to the close of polls) and such results shall be recorded on a form provided by the Secretary of State. Any such change in the boundaries of a precinct shall conform with the requirements of subsection (a) of Code Section 21-2-261.1. [Note: Subsection a is the 2,000 voters per precinct requirement.] [...]

SECTION 19. [...]

Additionally, during the seven days before and on the day of the first election following such change [in location of voting precinct], a notice of such change shall be posted on the previous polling place and at three other places in the immediate vicinity thereof. Each notice posted shall state the location to which the polling place has been moved and shall direct electors to the new location. At least one notice at the previous polling place shall be a minimum of four feet by four feet in size. [...]

SECTION 20C. [...]

At the top of each ballot for an election shall be printed in prominent type the words 'OFFICIAL BALLOT,' followed by the name and designation of the precinct for which it is prepared and the name and date of the election. [...]

SECTION 25. [...]

To be timely received, an application for an absentee-by-mail ballot shall be received by the board of registrars or absentee ballot clerk no later than 11 days prior to the primary, election, or runoff. [...]

SECTION 28. [...]

There shall be a period of advance voting that shall commence:

a) On the fourth Monday immediately prior to each primary or election; and

b) As soon as possible prior to a runoff from any general primary or election but no later than the second Monday immediately prior to such runoff and shall end on the Friday immediately prior to each primary, election or runoff. Voting shall be conducted beginning at 9:00 A.M. and ending at 5:00 P.M. on weekdays, other than observed state holidays, during such period and shall be conducted on the second and third Saturdays during the hours of 9:00 A.M. through 5:00 P.M. and, if the registrar or absentee ballot clerk so chooses, the second Sunday, the third Sunday, or both the second and third Sundays prior to a primary or election during hours determined by the registrar or absentee ballot clerk, but no longer than 7:00 A.M. through 7:00 P.M. [...]

[...] the registrars may extend the hours for voting to permit advance voting from 7:00 A.M. until 7:00 P.M. and may provide for additional voting locations pursuant to Code Section 21-2-382 to suit the needs of the electors of the jurisdiction at their option. [...]

SECTION 33. [...]

No person shall solicit votes in any manner or by any means or method, nor shall any person distribute or display any campaign material, nor shall any person give, offer to give, or participate in the giving of any money or gifts, including, but not limited to, food and drink, to an elector, nor shall any person solicit signatures for any petition, nor shall any person, other than election officials discharging their duties, establish or set up any tables or booths on any day in which ballots are being cast:

1) Within 150 feet of the outer edge of any building within which a polling place is established;

2) Within any polling place; or

3) Within 25 feet of any voter standing in line to vote at any polling place.

These restrictions shall not apply to conduct occurring in private offices or areas which cannot be seen or heard by such electors.

e) This Code section shall not be construed to prohibit a poll officer from distributing materials, as required by law, which are necessary for the purpose of instructing electors or from distributing materials prepared by the Secretary of State which are designed solely for the purpose of encouraging voter participation in the election being conducted or from making available self-service water from an unattended receptacle to an elector waiting in line to vote. [...]

SECTION 36. [...]

After the time for the closing of the polls and the last elector voting, the poll officials in each precinct shall complete the required accounting and related documentation for the precinct and shall advise the election superintendent of the total number of ballots cast at such precinct and the total number of provisional ballots cast. The chief manager and at least one assistant manager shall post a copy of the tabulated results for the precinct on the door of the precinct and then immediately deliver all required documentation and election materials to the election superintendent. The election superintendent shall then ensure that such ballots are processed, counted, and tabulated as soon as possible and shall not cease such count and tabulation until all such ballots are counted and tabulated.

b) The election superintendent shall ensure that each precinct notifies the election superintendent of the number of provisional ballots cast as soon as possible after the time for the closing of the polls and the last elector votes. The election superintendent shall post such information publicly. [...]

21-2-421

(a) As soon as possible but not later than 10:00 P.M. following the close of the polls on the day of a primary, election, or runoff, the election superintendent shall report to the Secretary of State and post in a prominent public place the following information:

1) The number of ballots cast at the polls on the day of a primary, election, or runoff, including provisional ballots cast;

2) The number of ballots cast at advance voting locations during the advance voting period for the primary, election, or runoff; and

3) The total number of absentee ballots returned to the board of registrars by the deadline to receive such absentee ballots on the day of the primary, election, or runoff. [...]

How does mandatory Saturday voting that wasn't previously guaranteed give voters *less* of an opportunity to vote? How is having the option of self-service water racist? How are shorter lines at the polls a form of voter discrimination? Is tabulating votes in a timely manner suppressing voters? Democrats...? Media...?

I hope you didn't get too bored reading the above text from Georgia SB 202. If you did, I don't blame you. At least you weren't as bored as I was when I read all 98 pages of the bill! I included a number of the most important parts of SB 202, but would encourage anyone to read directly from the primary source rather than relying on the media for information. Any honest and objective person can read SB 202 and understand that it is intended to make Georgia state elections smooth and fair by reducing wait time at the polls, adding mandatory Saturday voting, requiring ballots to be tabulated in a timely manner and reducing the chance of voter tampering. As the writers of SB 202 said, it needs to be "easy to vote and hard to cheat."

The following are a few media headlines about SB 202:

"Georgia's voter suppression bill is an assault on our democracy"

—Andre M. Perry and Anthony Barr, www.brookings.edu

"Georgia GOP Passes Major Law to Limit Voting"

—*New York Times*

"Georgia Republicans speed sweeping elections bill restricting voting access into law."

—CNN

"Biden calls new GOP-passed Georgia law restricting voting access an 'atrocity.'"

—ABC News

Speaking of the 46th President, here is his statement regarding SB 202:

"Instead of celebrating the rights of all Georgians to vote or winning campaigns on the merits of their ideas, Republicans in the state instead rushed through an un-American law to deny people the right to vote. This law, like so many others being pursued by Republicans in statehouses across the country is a blatant attack on the Constitution and good conscience. Among the outrageous parts of this new state law, it ends voting hours early so working people can't cast their vote after their shift is over. It adds rigid restrictions on casting absentee ballots that will effectively deny the right to vote to countless voters. And it makes it a crime to provide water to voters while they wait in line—lines Republican officials themselves have created by reducing the number of polling sites across the state, disproportionately in Black neighborhoods."

As anyone who reads SB 202 can see, everything in Biden's statement is completely false. This is the president of the United States! Can we hold this administration accountable, please?

★ ★ ★

Many corporations and celebrities were also very critical of the bill, with many signing an open letter condemning SB 202. The most drastic response was Major League Baseball moving their All-Star

Game from Atlanta to Denver—a move that many, from Joe Biden to LeBron James, approved of.

Estimates say that moving the MLB All-Star Game from Atlanta cost the city and its residents $70 to $100 million. Approximately 50 percent of Atlanta residents and 30 percent of business owners in the city are Black. In contrast, just under 10 percent of Denver's population is Black. This was a move supported by Democrats, Progressives, celebrities and woke corporations that cost the Black population living in the Atlanta area tens of millions of dollars.

If you have made it to this point, congratulations! The point is to consider what the bill actually reads versus what the media and celebrities say about it. Pay attention to the facts, not propaganda!

★ ★ ★

The 2022 Georgia primary election had a record voter turnout, completely debunking the bogus claims that the left and the media had made after SB 202 was passed. Over 1.9 million people cast their votes for both the governor and US Senate races in the May 2022 primary election. This was an increase of over 66 percent from the last primary election for governor in 2018 and over 115 percent from the last primary election for this senate seat in 2016. The increase was even greater for the early voting period, as there was a whopping 212 percent increase in votes (over 850,000 total) over the totals for the 2020 presidential primary and a 168 percent increase over the 2018 gubernatorial contest! The 2022 Georgia primary election was a huge success with the record turnout, shorter lines and easy ballot access at the polls. Remember, the left and the media said SB 202 would suppress Georgia voters. They were lying to you again!

Total Votes for Governor of Georgia (Primary Elections)

2018: 1,162,530

2022: 1,931,910

Total Votes for Georgia US Senate Seat (Primary Elections)

2016: 887,713

2022: 1,910,219

Here is Brad Raffensperger's statement on the record voter turnout in May of 2022:

> "The record early voting turnout is a testament to the security of the voting system and the hard work of our county election officials. The incredible turnout we have seen demonstrates once and for all that Georgia's Election Integrity Act struck a good balance between the guardrails of access and security."

★ ★ ★

The left has also been pushing the narrative that voter identification is racist. Let's look at some of the countries that require voter identification.

Canada	Sweden
Mexico	Norway
Brazil	Netherlands
Argentina	Iceland
Greece	France
Italy	

Are all of these countries racist...?

The Elections Canada website explains the requirements of voting in Canadian federal elections as such:

Option 1: Show one of these pieces of ID

- your driver's license
- any other card issued by a Canadian government (federal, provincial/ territorial or local) with your photo, name and current address

Option 2: Show two pieces of ID

Both must have your name and at least one must have your current address.

Examples:

- voter information card and bank statement
- utility bill and student ID card

Option 3: If you don't have ID

You can still vote if you declare your identity and address in writing and have someone who knows you and who is assigned to your polling station vouch for you.

The voucher must be able to prove their identity and address. A person can vouch for only one person.

In Mexico, voter IDs are also required. Instituto Nacional Electoral says the following concerning their photo-voting card:

The photo-voting card issued free of charge by the IFE to all citizens that have requested to be included in the electoral registry is an essential document to exercise the right to vote. In exceptional cases clearly foreseen by the law and for the purpose of voting within the national territory, a citizen who does not carry and show his/her photo-voting card on the day of the elections is not allowed to cast his/her vote.

In order to guarantee its reliability and inviolability, the IFE produces photo-voting cards using the information from the applications included in the Electoral Roll, in a centralized way and taking a number of security measures. The card is delivered to citizens about 20 days after submitting their application, and contains the following information:

- State, municipal section and city, which correspond to the home address of the voter.

- Electoral section where, as a rule, the voter living within the country should vote.

- Full name, address, gender and age of the citizen.

- Population Registration Code.

- Year of issuing and expiration.

Many of you have probably heard Bernie Sanders and other Democratic Socialists often reference and praise the Norwegian countries, in particular Sweden. These same democratic socialists also strongly oppose any form of voter ID, calling them words such as "burdensome" and "racist." As part of a tweet from October 2014, Bernie said this: "Voter ID laws aren't really intended to discourage fraud, they're intended to discourage voting." As of October 2022, Senator Sanders says he wants to "abolish burdensome voter ID laws" on his website.

Let's see if Sweden requires a voter ID. The following is text from a PDF of the Swedish Election Authority in regard to voter identification:

"If you are entitled to vote you will receive a voting card in the post, about three weeks before the elections. The voting card indicates which elections you are entitled to vote in, together with the name, address and opening hours of your polling station. On the voting card you will also find information about those venues where you can vote in advance. If you are going to vote in advance, you must bring your voting card. […]

In order to vote, you must be able to verify your identity by showing an ID document e.g. driving license or passport. If you have no ID document, another person may verify your identity, but in that case this person must be able to show an ID document. […]

You can only vote in the polling station that appears on your voting card. The polling station is only open on Election Day. When you vote at your polling station, your name is ticked off on the electoral roll, and your votes are placed in the ballot boxes."

Whoa…voter IDs *are* required in Sweden. Is Sweden guilty of voter discrimination? Is Sweden racist?

★ ★ ★

Leftists who claim the Scandinavian countries are socialist and should be a model for the US are either unaware or they are lying to you. The Index of Economic Freedom, which measures how capitalistic a country is based on regulation and taxation in the economy, ranks the Scandinavian countries at ten, eleven, and fourteen for the year 2022, while the US is ranked twenty-fifth out of the 177 countries listed. The countries ranked 146 or below are labeled as "repressed," with China listed at 158, Cuba at 175, Venezuela at 176 and North Korea at 177.

Rankings according to the Index of Economic Freedom, with number one being most free (or capitalistic) and number 177 being least free:

#10 Denmark	#35 Japan
#11 Sweden	#67 Mexico
#14 Norway	#175 Cuba
#15 Canada	#176 Venezuela
#19 South Korea	#177 North Korea
#25 United States	

Can someone please tell the Progressive left that Sweden is more capitalistic than the United States and that they require a voter ID?!

Can someone please tell the Progressive left that their policies resemble those of Cuba and Venezuela, not those of Sweden, Norway or Denmark?!

Yeah, I know—if you present a far leftist with facts, you'll most likely be called a bigot, a racist, told that you want to suppress voters or you don't know what you're talking about…

**The House Republicans who voted to object to the 2020 election results raised less than half of the donations from corporate groups in 2021 that they did in 2019, roughly $9 million down from about $19 million. The corporate donations for those House Republicans who did not object to the 2020 election results increased over the same span, as they received about $14 million in 2021 and $13 million in 2019. Over 120 Republican House members voted to object to the election results from Pennsylvania and Arizona, while smaller numbers voted to object to those in Michigan, Georgia and Nevada. **

The states and localities (generally counties) are responsible for running their own elections. Thus, election laws and procedures vary by state and county.

Chapter Ten

In the early 1990s, over half of Americans ranked crime as the country's biggest problem. This should come as no surprise to anyone who lived through the 1970s, 80s, early 90s or even someone who has taken the time to look up stats on violent crime. The total number of violent crimes—which the FBI classifies as murder, nonnegligent manslaughter, forcible rape, robbery and aggravated assault—hit all-time highs in the early 1990s, with over 1,900,000 offenses recorded in 1991, 1992 and 1993. Many of these were murders and nonnegligent manslaughters, totaling with 24,700 in 1991, 23,760 in 1992 and 24,530 in 1993. The number of murders in the early nineties had more than doubled, and the total number of violent crimes had increased by six times from those committed just three decades prior. In order to win the 1992 presidency and maintain popularity, Bill Clinton knew he would have to take a tougher stance on crime than Democrats had traditionally done.

H.R. 3355 (better known as the Clinton Crime Bill) was sponsored by Congressman Jack Brooks of Texas and first introduced in the House of Representatives in October of 1993. This bill remains the largest piece of criminal justice legislation in US history and had a tremendous impact in reducing violent crime. H.R. 3355 is 356 pages and consists of new legislation and funding geared toward crime fighting and prevention, including harsher penalties for crimes against women, sex offenders whose victims are below the age of sixteen, drug dealing in "drug-free zones," murder and other violent crimes. The bill authorized more than $30 billion over a six-year period: $10.8 billion for state and local law enforcement, $9.7 billion for prison construction, $7.1 billion for crime prevention and $2.6 billion for federal law enforcement. The legacy of the Clinton Crime Bill has been controversial, but the facts show that violent crime dropped significantly after its passage by Congress and signing into law by President Clinton in September of 1994.

Number of Recorded Murders/Nonnegligent Manslaughters by Year

1990: 23,440	2006: 17,309
1991: 24,700	2007: 17,128
1992: 23,760	2008: 16,465
1993: 24,530	2009: 15,399
1994: 23,330	2010: 14,722
1995: 21,610	2011: 14,661
1996: 19,650	2012: 14,856
1997: 18,210	2013: 14,319
1998: 16,974	2014: 14,164
1999: 15,522	2015: 15,883
2000: 15,586	2016: 17,413
2001: 15,980	2017: 17,294
2002: 16,229	2018: 16,374
2003: 16,528	2019: 16,669
2004: 16,148	2020: 21,570
2005: 16,740	2021: 22,900

The FBI had to estimate national crime figures for 2021 because many police agencies across the country (an estimated 40 percent) did not report their crime data to them. Some of these cities did not report any data, while others only reported partial data. This lack of reporting was apparently due to a change in the system the FBI uses to record crime stats, and even the nation's two largest cities, New York and Los Angeles, did not report any data, while the nation's third largest city, Chicago, only reported partial data.

The impact the Clinton Crime Bill had in reducing violent crime speaks for itself in the numbers. As you can see, murders substantially kicked back up in 2020 and 2021. What happened? Well, criminal justice reform—which might as well be called pro-criminal or anti-law enforcement reform—gained a lot of traction in the first part of the 2020s, both on a national level as well as on many local levels across the country. The spike in violent crime happened in 2020, but some dominoes were already in place for this to have happened. Rather than supporting the successful parts of the 1994 Crime Bill, Progressives have done exactly the opposite. Progressive district attorneys such as Kim Foxx in Chicago, Larry Krasner in Philadelphia, Chesa Boudin in San Francisco and George Gascón in Los Angeles have given a far left-wing philosophy precedence over their job of controlling violent crime and lawlessness in the cities they were elected to represent.

★ ★ ★

In Illinois, George Soros-backed Progressive prosecutor Kim Foxx was elected as Cook County State's Attorney in November of 2016 and Progressive billionaire J. B. Pritzker as governor in November of 2018. Both Foxx and Pritzker are advocates for "criminal justice reform."

According to the *Chicago Tribune*, 25,183 defendants had their felony charges dismissed in Foxx's first three years as state's attorney. This made up a total of 29.9 percent of all felony defendants—up from the 19.4 percent her predecessor, Anita Alvarez, dismissed in her last three years in this role. Not only is Foxx's office dropping charges more often than her predecessor, but it also has a lower overall conviction rate. Foxx's offices have a 66 percent conviction rate, which is 9 points lower than Alvarez had, even though Foxx claims she is more selective about the cases her office prosecutes. This chart shows a breakdown of dismissal rates under Fox and Alvarez:

	Homicide Cases	Sex Crimes	Aggravated Battery	Narcotics
Foxx:	8.1%	9.5%	7%	53.8%
Alvarez:	5.3%	6.5%	5.9%	34.5%

Kim Foxx was elected to a second term in November of 2020—an election in which George Soros contributed more than $2 million to the Illinois Justice and Safety PAC, which supported her re-election. Here is Foxx's tweet from the day she was sworn in for her second term in December of 2020:

> "Today I was sworn in to serve the people of Cook County as your State's Attorney for a second term. While there is still much work to do, and I cannot wait to get started, I'm immensely proud of the incredible strides we've made in just four short years."

Here is a list of those who have endorsed Kim Foxx, according to her website:

Mayor Lori Lightfoot

Governor J. B. Pritzker

US Senator Tammy Duckworth

US Senator Dick Durbin

US Senator Elizabeth Warren

US Senator Bernie Sanders

US Senator Kamala Harris

Cook County Democratic Party

Chicago Teachers Union

Yikes!

Many people in Chicago, including Police Superintendent Dave Brown, believe the number of violent offenders being released with electronic monitoring is to blame for the increased violence. In the first five months of 2021 alone, Cook County judges ordered electronic monitoring (as opposed to holding in jail) for violent offenders more than one thousand times, including 93 people charged with murder, 261 charged as armed habitual offenders, 534 charged as felons in possession of a weapon, and 569 charged with aggravated unlawful use of a weapon. This is in a city where the number of shooting victims increased from 2,596 in 2019 to 4,027 in 2020 and murders increased from 492 to 772.

Shooting Victims in Chicago	Criminal Homicides in Chicago
2019: 2,596	2019: 492
2020: 4,027	2020: 772
2021: 4,373	2021: 800

It gets worse! Chicago is the murder capital of America—in total homicides! From 2002 to 2014, there were 6,230 criminal homicides in the Windy City. This is 4,397 more than the 1,833 Americans who were killed in Afghanistan from late 2001 to 2014 and it still gets worse! In 2020 and 2021, there were 1,572 people killed in Chicago—an average of 786 per year and a 61 percent increase from the aforementioned thirteen-year period from 2002 to 2014, which averaged 479 criminal homicides annually.

It would have made sense for the Illinois state legislature and Governor Pritzker to "back the blue" and work with law enforcement to make sure they had the necessary resources to combat the sharp rise in crime in 2020, right? Well apparently not, because they did exactly the opposite…

★ ★ ★

In January of 2021, the majority Democrat Illinois General Assembly passed House Bill 3653, a sweeping 764-page criminal justice reform bill greatly impacting pretrial court processing (bail) and policing. House Bill 3653 eliminated cash bail by January 1, 2023, and allowed the courts to deviate away from mandatory minimum sentences. It also legislated that those under order of electronic monitoring or home detention are not guilty of an escape or violation unless they remain in violation for at least *forty-eight* hours!! What kind of trouble could an offender possibly get into in forty-eight hours?! Really?! HB 3653 also further increased suspects' rights upon detainment, allowing them to make three phone calls within three hours of arrival at the police station before questioning occurs and giving them the ability to retrieve phone numbers from their cell phones prior to it being placed in inventory.

These are just a few of the ways HB 3653 helps suspects and offenders. Now, what does it do to help law enforcement in Illinois? Well… nothing! It allows for complaints to be filed against law enforcement without a sworn affidavit or other legal documentation, stripping them of protections!

Pritzker signed the bill into law a month later in February of 2021. He said the following:

> "This legislation marks a substantial step toward dismantling the systemic racism that plagues our communities, our state and our nation and brings us closer to true safety, true fairness and true justice."

Kim Foxx tweeted this:

> "This is a historic day for Illinois. #HB3653 is what real criminal justice reform looks like. I'm proud to help support this bill, and I

am in awe of the hard work of the advocates, activists, and legislators that made this possible."

This new law has rightfully drawn a lot of criticism. The Illinois Law Enforcement Coalition made this statement:

"This new law is a blatant move to punish an entire, honorable profession that will end up hurting law-abiding citizens the most. Because we are sworn to protect and serve the public, we sincerely hope that we will not be proven right about this new law, that it won't cause police officers to leave the profession in droves and handcuff those who remain so they can't stop crimes against people and property. Please don't let us measure its dismal failure by the shattered lives it produces. We urge all citizens to remember who supported this law, and keep that in mind the next time they look to the police in Illinois for the protection they can no longer provide."

Not only has Pritzker signed into law this pro-criminal bill, but he doubled the state gas tax in 2019 (his first year in office) and is pushing to lower the state income tax refund for private school scholarship donors. The Illinois state gas tax increase was prompted by the $45 billion plan Pritzker signed into law in 2019 to fund improvement for infrastructure, which increased the tax from $0.19 to $0.38 per gallon.

As you should know and have already read about in this book (hopefully :)), Progressives want more government control. One of the major areas is in education. As of 2022, the state income tax refund for taxpayers who donate to private school scholarship funds receive a credit of $0.75 on the dollar for their donations. Pritzker wants to reduce this credit to $0.40 on the dollar, calling these tax credits "corporate tax loopholes" and saying they are unaffordable for the state.

The president of the scholarship granting organization Empower Illinois said "reducing it [the tax refund credit level] could threaten the lifeblood of the program. For us, over 80 percent of our donors are giving $10,000 or less. These are donors who are concerned that they're not going to be able to give in the same way, at the same level, in the same capacity with the reduced credit." According to Empower Illinois, more than twenty-two thousand scholarships have been awarded since the program began, with a majority going toward students of color. Remember, more private school scholarship money gives students and parents more control over their education, which is not what Democrats want.

In addition to having the murder capital of the country, Governor Pritzker presides over the state with the worst bond rating in the nation and the state with the second highest percentage of outbound moves for all of the first three years of his governorship, 2019 to 2021.

★ ★ ★

Equivalent to the national level, the increased violent crime in Chicagoland affects those in poorer neighborhoods (particularly the Black residents) the most. In 2021, 80 percent of those killed in Cook County were Black, over 14 percent were Latino and 88 percent were male. Many of the victims of these violent crimes are innocent.

On the afternoon of July 14, 2021, Pritzker was one of several governors who met with Joe Biden at the White House to talk about infrastructure. That same afternoon, back in Chicago, a seventy-three-year-old Vietnam veteran named Keith Cooper was killed in his Hyde Park neighborhood by two individuals in an attempted carjacking. The attack occurred after Mr. Cooper had stopped for groceries on the way to his daughter's house. According to police, the two carjackers demanded his vehicle then attacked him, repeatedly punching him in the head. The offenders (one was a confirmed male; the other was seventeen and referred to as "person") did not get his vehicle, but due to the attack, Mr. Cooper suffered a heart attack and was pronounced dead at the hospital. Keith Cooper was a Marine Corps veteran who had survived two combat tours in Vietnam.

I chose to mention Mr. Cooper, but anyone who follows crime in Chicago knows that he is just one of the many innocent people hurt or killed due to violence in the Windy City every week. The increased violent crime this decade is a direct result of policies and actions of Progressive Democrats, and it has greatly hurt those the leftists claim they are helping. Poorer and predominantly Black neighborhoods in cities like Chicago are home to many good people. These neighborhoods, however, have a percentage of the residents (generally younger males) who are in gangs, involved with drugs and are responsible for a large percentage of the crime in these communities. The majority of the residents are not out committing crimes. Progressive liberals say that the criminal justice system is racist against people of color, in particular Black people. While attempting to make the criminals the victims, the true (and majority Black) victims—the young, the old and the innocent—are increasingly hurt due to these radical policies and agendas. This leads to more innocent Black people getting hurt, which is in itself racist!

★ ★ ★

One would guess that when the newly elected vice president visited the murder capital of the nation, crime would be a main reason for her visit. Well…guess again! In March of 2021, VP Kamala Harris visited Chicago to focus on vaccine equity. Mayor Lori Lightfoot personally invited Harris to come to the Windy City to share with her the details of the "prioritized equity in the rollout of Covid vaccines." Remember, this is the same Kamala Harris who said just six months prior that she didn't trust what Donald Trump said about the vaccine. This vaccine Harris is now promoting, of course, is the same vaccine that was approved for emergency use and distribution under the Trump Administration!

While the vice president was in Chicago, she met up with Kim

Foxx and Lieutenant Governor Juliana Stratton at Brown Sugar Bakery to eat German chocolate cake and cupcakes. Did the trio discuss or come up with a solution to combat Chicago's violent crime? Based on the stats, I'm assuming not…

In the September 2018 Senate hearings for the nomination of Brett Kavanaugh to the Supreme Court, Kamala Harris took a strong stance against the future justice. Harris told Christine Blasey Ford, who accused Kavanaugh of sexual assault from an alleged and unproven incident in the early 1980s, that she believed her and that it was courageous for her to come forward. Harris claims to take a strong stance on violence against women and encourages victims to come forward. At the Generation Equality Forum in Paris in June of 2021, she said this:

> "Throughout my career, I have worked to protect women from violence and exploitation. I know what happens when women are supported. I know what happens when women are heard. When women are heard, whether that is in the courtroom, in the workplace, in the halls of government, or at the ballot box, democracy is more complete."

So, what about the woman that Jacob Blake was convicted of abusing?

★ ★ ★

Every cognizant adult in the United States who was alive in August or September of 2020 likely remembers the police shooting involving Jacob Blake in Kenosha, Wisconsin. Police were called to a situation where Blake, who had an open warrant in a domestic violence case, wrestled with police, got away, was told to stop, reached into his car and was told by police to drop the knife before he was shot several times by one of the officers. Some of you, however, probably only remember that he was shot in the back several times by an officer.

Police had filed charges, and an arrest warrant was issued against

Jacob Blake for felony sexual assault, trespassing and domestic abuse in May of 2020. According to records obtained by the *New York Post*, Blake broke into the home of the victim (whom he knew), sexually assaulted her with his finger and stole her car. The alleged victim cried as she made her statement and said Blake "penetrating her digitally caused her pain and humiliation and was done without her consent" and she was "very humiliated and upset by the sexual assault." She said Blake assaulted her around "twice a year when he drinks heavily."

What did the self-proclaimed protector of women, Kamala Harris, do? Well, after the incident when Blake was shot, she met with his family and praised them. She told reporters "they're an incredible family and what they've endured, and they just do it with such dignity and grace. And you know, they're carrying the weight of a lot of voices on their shoulders."

Harris also said her message to Blake's family was "to express concern for their well-being, and of course for their brother and their son's well-being. And to let them know that they have support."

Support? What about support for the victim?

According to Blake's attorney, Benjamin Crump, Kamala Harris told Blake that she was "proud of him"!

Forget the disastrous first twenty-one months of Kamala Harris's time as vice president. Forget her inability to solve border issues, crime issues, foreign policy issues, her struggle to answer basic questions, her nervous cackle, her obvious hatred of being challenged or even her inability to keep her staff. Forget all her incompetencies for a moment and ask yourself, "How can I trust anything she says ever again?"

★ ★ ★

Many in the professional sports world spoke or acted in protest due to the Blake incident. The Milwaukee Bucks, for example, issued a statement "calling for justice for Jacob Blake and demand the officers be held accountable." The team refused to come out of the locker room for their playoff game in protest. Soon after, the NBA announced it was suspending its playoff games for that night of August 26, 2020, as well as for the following night. The WNBA also suspended their games scheduled for August 26. ESPN2 broadcasted WNBA players from the six teams scheduled to play that night as they locked in arms and kneeled while wearing shirts spelling out the name of the accused and later convicted domestic abuser, Jacob Blake. Professional tennis player Naomi Osaka announced she would not play in the semifinals of the Western and Southern Open in Cincinnati. Osaka also wrote this: "Watching the continued genocide of Black people at the hand of the police is honestly making me sick to my stomach."

The Western and Southern Open ended up postponing its matches for August 27, 2020, and resuming them the next day.

Per usual, NBA player and self-proclaimed "king" and "cerebral" LeBron James spoke out regarding the Blake incident. If people weren't already tired of LeBron after his "decision" in 2010—his NBA Finals collapse where he got outplayed by Jason Terry and DeShawn Stevenson in the 2011 Finals—his repetitive flopping, or his history of stat padding after the game has been decided, they definitely were after hearing him talk about politics or criminal justice.

Don't believe me that people are tired of LeBron? Fine. Believe the viewer numbers! When LeBron tweets, he adds an emoji of a crown, signifying "king." Funny thing is, the NBA Finals ratings have been down since LeBron's teams have often been participants over the past decade. This viewership collapse has been even more drastic since 2020, when LeBron and many other NBA players, coaches, organizations, media members and the NBA itself began pushing their one-sided opinions on political and criminal justice issues, including such significant anti-police rhetoric.

The 1998 NBA Finals (Michael Jordan's final year with the Bulls) averaged 28.99 million viewers per game for that six-game series. The first year LeBron James won a championship in 2012, a per-game average of 16.85 million people tuned into that series. In 2020, however, a measly per game average of 7.53 million viewers tuned in to watch LeBron's Lakers in the finals.

The 2019 and 2021 NBA Finals, in which LeBron's teams did not play, averaged more viewers than his before mentioned 2020 team—15.13 and 9.89 million, respectively. In theory, more people had an opportunity to watch the finals in 2020 due to Covid-related employer shutdowns, but they chose not to tune in to see LeBron.

NBA Finals Average Number of Viewers (in millions)

1998: 28.99	2020: 7.53
2012: 16.85	2021: 9.89
2019: 15.13	

A little arrogant for LeBron to call himself the "king" when the NBA Finals ratings have collapsed by over three times from the end of the Jordan Era to the end of the LeBron Era, don't ya think?!

LeBron James is one of the many NBA players, coaches and personalities that viewers have become tired of and feel insulted by. Most fans want to be able to simply enjoy the games without the NBA and many of its biggest personalities lecturing you, the viewer. As the ratings indicate, many viewers are too smart and too proud to turn on the television and watch professional athletes protesting the same country in which they were able to take advantage of their opportunity to have fortune and fame.

★ ★ ★

On the subject of basketball, remember the three UCLA basketball players who were arrested for shoplifting in China in November of 2017? The three players, LiAngelo Ball, Cody Riley and Jalen Hill, were arrested for allegedly stealing sunglasses from a Louis Vuitton store in Hangzhou. People arrested in China don't have the same legal protections as those arrested in the US, and the young men were potentially facing three to ten years in prison. After the incident, President Trump spoke with Chinese President Xi Jinping and asked him to help resolve this case. About a week later, Ball, Riley and Hill were allowed to return to the US. The three thanked Donald Trump for intervening in the incident.

Over four years later, in February of 2022, WNBA Phoenix Mercury star Brittney Griner was detained in Russia and kept in custody for having vape cartridges with marijuana concentrate in her luggage. In August of 2022, Griner was convicted and sentenced to nine years in Russian prison. Yes, nine years! How absurd is that? What is also very absurd is that so many in the professional basketball world (and in general) protest America rather than acknowledging the great country it is and the opportunity it has!

The US and Russia have been in negotiations about possible prisoner swaps to bring Griner home. Will this happen? We don't know, but as of October 2022, Griner is still in Russian prison. Whether or not you like Trump, Americans both at home and abroad were much safer when the 45th President was in office than after the 46th entered.

★ ★ ★

Now, back to LeBron's comments on Jacob Blake. I know you must be going crazy to hear what the self-proclaimed "king" said.

"We are scared as Black people in America. Black men, Black women, Black kids, we are terrified.

If you're sitting here telling me that there was no way to sadue that gentleman or detain him before the firing of guns, then you're sitting here lying not only to me, but you're lying to every African American, every Black person in the community."

Wrong, LeBron!

The bystander who recorded the video of the Blake incident said he saw police wrestling with the man (Blake) and an officer fire a stun gun at him. He also heard police yell, "Drop the knife!" before shots were fired.

It was later confirmed by both the Kenosha County District Attorney and the United States Justice Department that officers did try to subdue Blake, including shocking him three different times with their Tasers, all attempts being ineffective.

The following are the factual and legal conclusions from the Kenosha County District Attorney:

> "On Sunday, August 23, 2020, at approximately 5:10 pm, Laquisha Booker, the mother of Jacob Blake's children, called the police reporting that Jacob Blake had taken the keys to her rental vehicle which he would not return to her. Laquisha Booker stated that she was afraid that Jacob Blake was going to take her vehicle and crash it as, she stated, he had done before.

> As a result of this call, Officer Sheskey, Officer Meronek, and Officer Arenas were dispatched to Laquisha Booker's residence located at 2805 40th St. in the City of Kenosha.

> Responding officers were told that this was a "family trouble" call involving a dispute over car keys between Jacob Blake and the mother of his children.

> Jacob Blake had a felony warrant for his arrest.

The involved officers knew Jacob Blake had a felony warrant for his arrest and knew that the warrant involved domestic violence charges and a sexual assault charge.

Officer Sheskey obtained a description of Jacob Blake and knew he would have to arrest Jacob Blake on the warrant if he encountered him.

When officers arrived, Laquisha Booker flagged them down and shouted statements identifying Jacob Blake as the other person involved and indicating that he was trying to take her car, stating, "My kids are in the car."

Officer Sheskey saw Jacob Blake and saw him putting a child in the back of the vehicle in question, a gray Dodge SUV.

Officer Sheskey immediately attempted to arrest Jacob Blake based on his active warrant and was quickly assisted by Officer Arenas and Officer Meronek.

Jacob Blake knew there was a warrant out for his arrest.

Jacob Blake did not comply with the verbal commands of officers as they attempted to arrest him.

When the officers attempted to physically restrain Jacob Blake, he resisted, physically struggling with officers.

Officers brought Jacob Blake to the ground, but he was able to get off the ground and to get away from the officers trying to arrest him.

During this struggle, Officer Sheskey and Officer Arenas both attempted to subdue Jacob Blake by deploying their tasers.

Both times that Jacob Blake was struck with the tasers, he ripped out the taser wires/prongs making the tasers ineffective against him.

Officer Sheskey also attempted to drive stun Jacob Blake with his taser by applying the taser to Jacob Blake's neck/back area, but that too was ineffective.

As he resisted arrest, Jacob Blake was armed with a knife.

By the time he was walking in front of the SUV, the knife was opened and the blade was exposed.

Jacob Blake did not comply with police commands to drop the knife.

Jacob Blake tried to enter the driver's door of the SUV.

The SUV had been rented by Laquisha Booker in her name and Laquisha Booker had indicated to police that Jacob Blake did not have permission to drive the vehicle.

There were children in the SUV who Laquisha Booker had yelled were her children.

Jacob Blake had the opened knife in his right hand and was attempting to escape from Officer Sheskey's grasp and enter the driver's side of the SUV.

Both Officer Sheskey and Officer Arenas stated that in the moment before Officer Sheskey opened fire, Jacob Blake twisted his body, moving his right hand with the knife towards Officer Sheskey.

Two citizen witnesses saw Jacob Blake's body turn in a manner that appears consistent with what the officers described.

Officer Sheskey shot Jacob Blake seven times in total. There were four entrance wounds to Jacob Blake's back and three entrance wounds to his left side (flank).

Officer Sheskey stated that he fired shots until Jacob Blake dropped the knife. Noble Wray explained this is consistent with law enforcement training where officers are instructed to continue shooting until they stop the threat.

With these facts established, I do not believe the State could prove beyond a reasonable doubt that Officer Sheskey was not acting lawfully in self-defense or defense of others which is the legal standard the State would have to meet to obtain a criminal conviction in this case. I also do not believe that there are any viable criminal charges against Officer Maronek or Officer Arenas neither of whom fired a shot in this case.*"*

There ya go, Kamala. There ya go, LeBron. There ya go, athletes and celebrities—these are the facts…

In November of 2020, Blake and the prosecution came to a plea deal in which he pleaded guilty to two counts of disorderly conduct and domestic abuse and was sentenced to two years of probation. In the deal, one count of criminal trespassing and one count of third-degree sexual assault and domestic abuse were dropped. After investigations were complete, it was determined that Officer Sheskey would not face discipline within the department and returned to work in March of 2021. Kenosha Police Chief Miskinis made the following statement: "He [Officer Sheskey] was found to have been acting within policy and will not be subjected to discipline."

When speaking of the video of the Blake shooting posted on social media, James also said, "I think firearms are a huge issue in America. […] They're not used just for hunting that a lot of people do for sport. Right now for Black people, right now when you're hunting, we think you're hunting us."

★ ★ ★

The 2020s have started off as a very dangerous decade for police. In 2021, 346 police officers were shot in the line of duty, 63 of whom were killed. This is up from 312 shot in 2020 with 47 killed and 293 shot in 2019 with 50 killed. Ambush attacks on officers in 2021 were up 115 percent from 2020, with 103 separate ambush-style attacks and 130 officers shot.

One of these ambush shootings occurred in the Los Angeles suburb of Compton, less than three weeks after LeBron's comment "We think you're hunting us." On September 12, 2020, two Los Angeles County

Sheriff's deputies were sitting in their patrol car when a lone gunman approached the vehicle and opened fire, hitting both the male and female deputies inside. The gunman approached from behind the patrol car, walked along its side as if he were going to pass it and opened fire. Both deputies suffered multiple gunshot wounds and fortunately did later recover from their injuries.

The suspect, a Black male named Deonte Lee Murray, was charged for the shootings later that month. Murray was already being held on bond for $1 million for felony counts of carjacking, second-degree robbery and assault with a semiautomatic firearm for a September 1, 2020 carjacking in which he allegedly shot a man in the leg with a high-powered rifle and stole his black Mercedes. There is strong evidence that Murray is the ambush shooter of the officers, including ballistic and forensic evidence from the gun used in the attack and the black Mercedes fleeing the scene. Murray has an extensive criminal history that includes convictions for sales of narcotics, firearm possession by a felon, burglary and terrorist threats. Upon being charged for shooting the deputies, Murray's bail increased from just over $1 million to $6.15 million. He initially pleaded not guilty to the new charges.

In Chicago, over seventy people were shot and ten killed during the weekend of August 6–8, 2021. One of the deaths was CPD Officer Ella French. Officer French and her partner were executing a traffic stop for expired tags around nine p.m. that Saturday evening, an evening which quickly turned deadly.

During the stop, the driver of the vehicle, Erik Morgan, was instructed to exit the vehicle. Upon doing so, he handed the keys to police and fled, causing one of the three officers at the scene to chase him. A struggle ensued with a second occupant—Erik's brother, Emonte Morgan—leading Officer French to help her partner in the chaos. Emonte Morgan, who had a gun in his waistband, shot Officer French and her partner, killing French and badly wounding her partner, whom he shot three times. The third officer heard the shots and was running back to the scene when the gunman started shooting at him. The officer returned fire and hit Emonte Morgan. Erik Morgan was caught and held by neighbors until police took him into custody—he also had a gun. Even with the struggle and imminent danger, both Ella French and her partner had their guns holstered.

Both Morgans were remanded. The man charged with supplying the handgun used in the shootings, however, was not. Jamel Danzy, an Indiana resident who was charged with providing the firearm used to kill Officer French and shoot her partner, was granted bail of only $4,500. Danzy was accused of buying the gun from a licensed dealer in Hammond, Indiana, and providing it to Morgan, whom he knew could not buy or possess firearms due to a felony conviction. He was charged with conspiracy to violate federal firearm laws and released on $4,500 bail by Judge Jeffrey Gilbert.

Danzy, who had apparently been in a relationship with Eric Morgan for three years, also was the owner of the vehicle the Morgans were driving the night of the murder. Danzy was not in the vehicle that night and said he felt bad about what happened. Many officers, including Chicago Police Chief David Brown, were very upset with Judge Gilbert's decision.

> "By allowing Mr. Danzy to walk free, the court has done a disservice to Officer French's memory, to the entire Chicago Police Department, and to the thousands of men and women across the country who work around the clock, day in and day out to stem the violence that is plaguing our communities.
>
> This decision sets a dangerous precedent that straw purchasers like Danzy are not a danger to society, despite the fact that his alleged actions directly led to the murder of a Chicago police officer and left another in critical condition."
>
> —Police Chief Brown

Officer Ella French served the city of Chicago courageously and was very well-liked by her fellow officers and those in the community. Just over a month prior to her death, she was one of the officers who rushed a one-month-old gunshot victim to the hospital after the infant had been shot in the head. Ella French played a large part in saving the young victim's life as she took her to a gurney in the emergency room and never left her side. The young victim's uncle stated how kind and comforting Officer French had been to his niece.

Ella French was one of seventy-six officers in the city of Chicago who were either shot or shot at in 2021, up from twenty-two fired upon just two years prior. The chart below shows the drastic uptick of people shooting at Chicago police officers in recent years.

Year	Officers Shot at in Chicago	Officers Hit by Gunfire in Chicago
2018	20	5
2019	22	5
2020	80	10
2021	76	16

★ ★ ★

LeBron James's comments in regard to the Jacob Blake incident was just one of the many times he ignored the facts and passed along propaganda while attempting to address criminal justice issues.

In April of 2021 in Columbus, Ohio, there was a violent altercation between young women leading to the police-involved shooting death of sixteen-year-old Ma'Khia Bryant. Bryant—who was armed with a knife and swinging it at another young woman, Shai-onta Craig—was shot by police after not responding to police commands to stop. Fearing for the life of Craig, the responding officer, Nicholas Reardon, shot and killed Bryant.

After the incident, LeBron tweeted a photo of Officer Reardon along with the caption "YOU'RE NEXT #ACCOUNTABILITY" with an hourglass emoji.

After receiving backlash, LeBron deleted his original tweet and posted another:

> "I'm so damn tired of seeing Black people killed by police. I took the tweet down because its being used to create more hate -This isn't about one officer. it's about the entire system and they always use our words to create more racism. I am so desperate for more ACCOUNTABILITY"

What about Black people killing other Black people, LeBron? The truth is that Officer Reardon likely saved the life of a Black girl. What should he have done, let Ms. Bryant stab Ms. Craig? It is unfortunate a life was lost that day, but Officer Reardon was doing his job as a protector of the community. LeBron was the one trying to pass along hate by making this incident about race, not facts!

After a full review of the shooting, Officer Reardon was cleared of any criminal wrongdoing.

> "Under Ohio law the use of deadly force by a police officer is justified when there exists an immediate or imminent threat of death or serious bodily injury to the officer or another."

—Special Prosecutors H. Tim Merkle and Gary Shroyer

★ ★ ★

We should be asking why we never hear of LeBron (and others) speaking out about Black-on-Black crime. Most homicide victims are killed by others of their same race. Between 1980 and 2008, the US Department of Justice found that 84 percent of White victims were killed by White offenders and 93 percent of Black victims were killed by Black offenders. In 2017, the FBI reported that 80 percent of White victims were killed by White offenders and 88 percent of Black victims were killed by Black offenders. In 2018, they reported 81 percent of White victims and 89 percent of Black victims were killed by others of their same race. In 2017, 16 percent of White victims were killed by Black offenders, and only 8 percent of Black victims were killed by White offenders. The narrative that leftists are trying to make doesn't line up with the facts!

Year 2017

White Victims Killed by White Offenders	Black Victims Killed by Black Offenders	White Victims Killed by Black Offenders	Black Victims Killed by White Offenders
80%	88%	16%	8%

★ ★ ★

The previously mentioned city of Chicago is the murder capital of the US, but there were several major US cities that saw record-breaking numbers of violent crime in 2021. Philadelphia, Austin, Columbus, Indianapolis, Portland, Memphis, Louisville, Milwaukee, Albuquerque and Saint Paul all had a record number of homicides in 2021, with Minneapolis tying its previous record.

Philadelphia had the most homicides of any city not named Chicago in 2021, totaling 562, with 2,326 total shooting victims that year. The "City of Brotherly Love" surpassed its previous yearly homicide record of 500 set in 1990 and had a 63 percent increase over its 2019 total of 353. Eighty percent of all those murdered were Black, with young males accounting for the most deaths. One of the victims was a pregnant thirty-two-year-old who was gunned down in front of her home as she was unloading gifts from her baby shower. The young mother, Jessica Covington, was shot in the head and multiple times in her abdomen. Both she and her baby were killed. Ms. Covington was seven months pregnant.

Far-left cities on the West Coast have had no shortage of violent crime and lawlessness either. If the tens of millions of dollars lost due to rioting and looting in Portland wasn't bad enough, the shootings and homicides skyrocketed too! Portland had an all-time record number of homicides in 2021, totaling 88—a 61 percent increase over the 2020 total of 55 and a 150 percent increase from the 2019 total of 36. The city recorded a total of 1,314 shooting incidents in 2021, up from 920 in 2020 and a whopping 219 percent increase from the 413 recorded in 2019!

Year	Homicides in Portland	Shooting Incidents in Portland
2019	36	413
2020	57	920
2021	88	1,314

Six hundred and thirty miles to the south, San Francisco is also no stranger to increased crime, lawlessness and decay. The "City by the Bay" had 56 homicides in 2021, up from 48 in 2020 and 41 in 2019. The city also recorded 222 victims of gun violence in 2021, up from 167 in 2020 and a 62 percent increase from the 137 in 2019!

Remember hearing about the spring 2021 heinous unprovoked stabbings of two older Asian women in San Francisco? The women, aged sixty-five and eighty-five, were stabbed by a man with an extensive history of violent crime. This occurred on May 4, 2021 by a man named Patrick Thompson, who calmly approached the elderly victims, violently stabbed them both and casually walked away. The eighty-five-year-old victim was stabbed with so much force, the knife blade broke off from the handle and remained in her body. Thompson was arrested about an hour after the attack and allegedly later told police that he had "no regrets."

Thompson has a criminal history including residential burglary, possession for sale of cocaine base, battery with serious bodily injury, and assault with a deadly weapon. One of the charges for assault with a deadly weapon occurred at a homeless shelter in 2017 and was witnessed by a former security guard who described the incident as follows:

> "He [the victim] was just laying on the bed and he [Thompson] came up and stabbed him with the scissors right in the chest. The look on his face was unbelievable. At the time so calm and very violent and he tried to push him out the window. He was halfway out the window."

The former security guard, Benjamin Gonzalez, restrained Thompson until police arrived after this 2017 attack. Thompson was supposed to be behind bars for twenty-five years to life for those charges but was released on mental health diversion in the fall of 2020.

San Francisco District Attorney Chesa Boudin actually asked that Thompson be held in jail for the spring 2021 stabbing of the Asian women, a request that the judge granted. Deputy Public Defender Eric Fleischaker conceded that there was evidence of the attack occurring but argued evidence of intent, stating, "You have to have a criminal mindset to be guilty of these offenses and Mr. Thompson was not in his right mind. He did not have access to the services and care that he needed at that time."

Unbelievable...

Mental health issues are real, but they should never override public safety!

This attack received national attention—possibly because it was caught on video, possibly because the victims were elderly and Asian. Violent crimes such as these *should* receive national attention. It needs to be exposed that innocent people get hurt when violent people with violent histories are labeled as "victims" and not held accountable for their actions. All too often, the police do their job and take a violent criminal off the street only to see them released by Progressive district attorneys or judges who sometimes in fairness have their "hands tied" by the law or political pressure. And yet, the police are the ones so many people try to vilify. Why has it become the norm for celebrities, much of the media and Progressive politicians to demonize the police, make heroes out of the criminals and forget about the victims?

Chesa Boudin was recalled by San Francisco voters on June 7, 2022, by around 22,000 votes, 122,588 to 100,177. Many voters of far-left San Francisco felt that Boudin's policies were to blame for the increased crime and quality of life decline in the city.

Memphis and Detroit had the highest per capita murder rates among large US cities in 2021.

★ ★ ★

Rather than proposing legislation to reduce crime in his first year as president, Biden supported legislation that would have increased it even more! H.R. 1280, also known as the George Floyd Justice in Policing Act of 2021, was introduced by Democrat Representative Karen Bass of California in February of 2021 and passed in the House almost exclusively along party lines just over a week later. Among other things, H.R. 1280 would have lowered the criminal intent standard—from "willful" to "reckless"—to convict a law enforcement officer for misconduct in a federal prosecution, limited qualified immunity as a defense to liability in a private civil action against a law enforcement officer, and granted administrative subpoena power to the DOJ.

Ok, first of all…police do not have qualified immunity when it comes to a criminal act. The fact that Derek Chauvin was convicted of murdering George Floyd proves this. People (or their families) can sue the city where misconduct or alleged misconduct by an officer occurs. The $27 million settlement the city of Minneapolis agreed to pay George Floyd's family in response to their lawsuit proves this. Qualified immunity is what exempts law enforcement officers from *personal* suits. Therefore, situations could arise where a police officer is cleared of any criminal wrongdoing, but someone takes them to civil court and sues the officer for their personal property. Eliminating qualified immunity for the police is simply stripping law enforcement officers of legal protection, which makes the job less desirable. All this would have accomplished is to cause more law enforcement officers to leave and fewer to start—leading to more crime across the country!

This is the March 1, 2021, statement from the White House regarding H.R. 1280:

> "To make our communities safer, we must begin by rebuilding trust between law enforcement and the people they are entrusted

to serve and protect. We cannot rebuild that trust if we do not hold police officers accountable for abuses of power and tackle systemic misconduct—and systemic racism—in police departments.

President Biden has a long record of championing meaningful policing reform and previously called for the Congress to enact provisions like those in H.R. 1280, the George Floyd Justice in Policing Act of 2021. The Administration encourages the House to pass this legislation, and looks forward to working with the Congress to enact a landmark policing reform law."

This statement by the Biden White House is incredibly phony, given a large part of Biden's campaign in running for president was creating distrust between law enforcement and the people in the communities they serve.

The National Education Association (NEA) submitted a letter to the House of Representatives on March 1, 2021, titled "Pass the George Floyd Justice in Policing Act (HR 1280)." The letter can be read in its entirety on the National Education Association's website. The first two paragraphs and the last two are as follows:

"**Dear Representative**:

On behalf of the 3 million members of the NEA across the nation who are dedicated to teaching, supporting, and nurturing all students regardless of their race or ethnicity, we urge you to vote YES on the George Floyd Justice in Policing Act of 2021 (H.R. 1280) and work to continue to improve the legislation. Votes associated with this issue may be included in NEA's Report Card for the 117th Congress.

Educators believe that preparing students for the responsibility of citizenship means teaching them to appreciate a fundamental principle of our democracy: Under our nation's system of laws, all of us are equal and deserving of protections. However, the recent police killings of George Floyd, Breonna Taylor, Rayshard Brooks, and Daniel Prude make a mockery of that principle, and have brought to the fore systemic, deeply rooted racism. In many communities of color, residents are not treated or policed according to the principle of equality under the law. They are not first viewed as citizens, but as suspects. [...]

NEA members are active in the fight for social and racial justice because it is directly linked to ensuring all students, in every community, have access to the learning opportunities they deserve. But these opportunities are only accessible to the extent that we keep students in Black and brown communities safe from police brutality and excessive use of force.

Protestors from coast to coast and even across the globe are pushing America to live up to our ideals and keep our promises; in fact, a recent study by Civis Analytics reported that the huge outpouring for Black lives may be the largest social justice movement ever in our nation. We are at an inflection point; we must not risk the possibility that another Black family will be left to mourn a loved one's senseless death at the hands of those we are supposed to trust. We urge you to join this movement for equal justice by voting YES on the George Floyd Justice in Policing Act, and we look forward to working with members of Congress in both chambers to improve the legislation and enact meaningful reforms. "

The Biden Administration and the NEA are not addressing or acknowledging the main problem. The main problem is not police committing violence against Black people; it is Black people committing violence against other Black people. Until our leaders are honest with addressing this issue, it will not improve.

Here are the facts: There are approximately 1,000 people shot and killed by police per year. In 2021, there were 1,055 recorded, in which Black people accounted for 27 percent. This means approximately 285 Black people were shot and killed by police in 2021. While accounting for 13 percent of the US population, approximately 53 percent of all murder victims are Black. In 2021, there were an estimated 22,900 murders/non-negligent manslaughters in the US. This number is probably low, but we'll use it. So, in line with the stats, approximately 12,137 Black people were murdered in 2021. Approximately 90 percent of Black people who are murdered in the US are murdered by other Black people. Based on these facts, an estimated 10,923 Black people were killed by other Black people- over 38 times higher than the number killed by police. Something else that needs to be pointed out is that we hear of very few police involved shootings or incidents where there is misconduct, meaning the vast majority are justified.

The goal here is not to demonize Black people in any way; it is simply to point out the facts and hopefully find a solution. Poverty drives crime, and children born into a safe community with a good family structure have a better chance of getting a good education and a lesser chance of becoming involved with crime. Young men are also very impressionable and need proper guidance, safe schools and safe after-school activities. The Democrats have been able to count on the Black vote for decades. Given the struggles predominantly Black communities with elected Democrats have faced, I don't see what there is to lose for these residents to vote in a different direction...

H.R. 1280 did not come up for a vote in the Senate, as it would have fallen well short of the sixty votes needed to pass the upper chamber. If H.R. 1280 had passed, it certainly would have led to more violent crime that would have in turn affected Black people at a disproportionate rate. The Biden Administration, Democrat politicians across the country, much of the media, celebrities and organizations such as the NEA continue to ignore these facts that have led to more people getting murdered every year—the majority by those in their same communities.

★ ★ ★

It is true the criminal justice system often is not fair. It is not always fair in regard to wealth, politics or principle. It isn't fair when a wealthy person can post bail for the same crime a poor person can't. A case being handled a certain way because of political pressure often isn't fair. District attorneys and public defenders both work for the same jurisdiction (or employer) and may feel the same pressure to handle a case a certain way, whereas a private attorney may not feel this. It isn't fair when a seventeen-year-old kills someone and gets off *easy,* knowing he or she won't be prosecuted as harshly. Attorneys often work out deals to avoid taking cases to trial—which can lead to a reduced sentence for a violent offender or even a potentially innocent person going to jail for some time to avoid the chance of a harsher sentence.

Of all the facets of the criminal justice system, law enforcement officers generally make up the most fair component. Peace officers do have legal authority on the streets, but once the suspect is in custody, they have virtually no control over the next steps in the criminal justice system. The vast majority of the time, suspects are taken into custody without major incident, and police-involved shootings that are not justified are incredibly rare. Again, all you have to do is look at the stats!!

Law enforcement officers go to work never knowing whether they are going to be a target of violence, what they are going to encounter during a vehicle stop or who is going to have a "dirty" needle or fentanyl in their possession. A large number of Democrat politicians, celebrities, corporations and much of the media have been very unfair toward police in the first few years of the 2020s. Although there is a level of justice needed for victims of crime and their families, the main goal of the criminal justice system should be public safety. The aforementioned facts discussed in this chapter have only created a less safe society.

★ ★ ★

Unfair treatment, fear and anti-police legislation passed by Democrats have made careers in law enforcement more difficult and less desirable. The Chicago Police Department had 908 vacancies as of January 2022 in addition to 614 more that were wiped out of the 2021 budget, totaling more than 1,500 positions. In Philadelphia, the Department was down 440 officers as of early 2022. In late 2021, Portland had 789 sworn officers—127 vacancies short of the 916 budgeted positions and the fewest of any point over the last thirty years, even with the city gaining more than 165,000 new residents during that time. San Francisco was short nearly 600 officers as of April 2022, and staffing has been steadily declining over the past three years.

Releasing violent offenders and attempting to criminalize police and decriminalize criminals does not work, people! How many more people need to die before we can figure this out? Once more: all you have to do is look at the crime stats!! We need to **fund** our local city, county and state police and **defund** DC!!

★ ★ ★

Another misleading tale the left tells is that high crime is a "red state" problem. It is true that several of the states with the highest per capita murder rates are, in fact, conservative states, but the largest percentage of violent crime occurring in those states is in metropolitan areas controlled by the left. For example, the state of Missouri had 738 recorded murders/non- negligent homicides in 2020. The two most populous cities, Kansas City and Saint Louis, had a total of 442—179 and 263, respectively. These two cities had a combined population of approximately 810,000 according to the 2020 census, while the state of Missouri had a total population of 6,155,000. So, based on the facts, Kansas City and Saint Louis accounted for 60 percent of the total murders in the state while only making up 13 percent of the state's total population. Do you think the mayors of these two cities are Democrat or Republican? Which political party do you think dominates the city councils? Which political party do you suspect the district attorneys belong to? You guessed it! All controlled by Democrats.

If you remove Saint Louis and Kansas City from Missouri, the state would have had the twenty-seventh highest murder rate in 2020, rather than where it stood at number two. Let's take it a step further and consider the 116 murders that occurred in Saint Louis County in 2020. The factuality is that 558 of the 738 murders recorded in Missouri that year occurred in Kansas City, Saint Louis City or Saint Louis County, which only comprise 29 percent of the state's population. Without the aforementioned three areas included, Missouri would have ranked thirty-third among the fifty states in per capita murder rate for the year 2020.

Murder Rates (2020)

	Saint Louis City	Kansas City	St. Louis County	Rest of State
Murders	263	179	116	180
Population (2020)	301,574	507,971	1,004,310	4,341,065
Rate per 100K People	87.20	35.23	11.5	4.1

Next, let's look at Tennessee. The city of Memphis led the state with 290 murders in 2020. For the same year, there were a total of 699 in the entire state of Tennessee, which had a 2020 population of 6,887,000. The 2020 population of Memphis was 631,539. This means the city of Memphis accounted for 42 percent of the state's murders while comprising only 9 percent of the state's population. Without Memphis included, Tennessee would have had the twenty-third highest murder rate in 2020, rather than the seventh. Even worse, Memphis ended up breaking its previous murder record two years in a row, with 290 in 2020 and 304 in 2021.

The city of Saint Louis is an independent city that operates both as a city and a county. Its population is not included in Saint Louis County.

Which political party runs the city of Memphis? You guessed it again! Anyone who takes the time to look up the stats will see more of the same in New Orleans, Jackson, Mississippi and on and on and on.

Murder Rates (2020)

	Memphis	Rest of Tennessee
Murders	290	409
Population (2020)	631,539	6,255,461
Rate per 100K People	45.91	6.53

Now let's look at a previously mentioned blue state! Illinois had the eighth highest murder rate among the fifty states in 2020. The Democrats have the governor's office and super majorities in both chambers of the legislature due to the heavily populated Chicagoland area, but the majority of Illinois is rural, leans conservative and does not have high levels of violent crime. If Chicago was not included when factoring the murder rate in Illinois, the state would have ranked thirty-six per capita in 2020.

Taking out the higher-crime cities of East Saint Louis, Kankakee, Danville, Rockford, Rock Island, Decatur, as well as the whole of Cook County, Illinois would have had a per capita murder rate of 2.84 intentional homicides per 100,000 residents in 2020—the sixth lowest in the nation. In addition, 68 of the 82 counties in Illinois that are classified as rural did not have a single murder in 2020. If these 82 rural counties made up their own state, they would have had the lowest murder rate of any state in the entire nation other than New Hampshire.

See a trend here? I think it's more than fair to say that your conservative, pro-Second Amendment Midwesterners who occupy most of rural Illinois and Missouri are not running around killing people in high numbers with their legally obtained and registered guns.

Murder Rates (2020)

	Illinois	Chicago	Rural Illinois Counties
Murders	1166	772	27
Population (2020)	12,812,545	2,746,352	2,009,049
Rate per 100K People	8.71	28.11	1.34

★ ★ ★

What do far-left politicians do when their cities are short on police officers and more dangerous people are on the streets? You guessed it—they spend more taxpayer dollars on their private security!

San Francisco Mayor London Breed announced in a press conference in July of 2020 that the city would be redirecting $120 million in funding from law enforcement agencies to addressing disparities in the Black community.

> "With this budget, we are listening to the community and prioritizing investments in the African American community around housing, mental health and wellness, workforce development, economic justice, education, advocacy and accountability."
>
> —Mayor London Breed

While Breed supports allocating money away from law enforcement, or defunding the police, she certainly didn't short her own taxpayer-paid security funds. Between 2015 and 2020, the city spent $12.4 million to protect the mayor. As the crime increased, so did the cost of Mayor Breed's security detail. It increased over 600 percent, actually—from $417,489 spent in 2016 to $2.6 million in 2020!

★ ★ ★

Most of us aren't able to use taxpayer money to beef up our personal security like London Breed has, but that hasn't stopped tens of millions of Americans from increasing their own. We did this by purchasing firearms, with a large percentage of the sales driven by first-time gun owners. In fact, 2020 and 2021 had record gun sales, with almost 21.6 million sold in 2020 and over 18.8 million in 2021. Almost 14 million of the approximately 40.5 million guns purchased were by first-time gun buyers—8.4 million in 2020 and 5.4 million in 2021.

Estimated Number of Guns Sold in the US per Year

2000:	7,515,608	2018:	13,467,578
2005:	8,017,173	2019:	13,492,224
2010:	10,025,191	2020:	21,593,355
2015:	14,835,847	2021:	18,860,450

There was a 62 percent increase in gun sales from 2019 to 2020! Why? Simple—people were fearful! People were (and still are) scared of the increased violent crime, lawlessness, calls to defund police and mass failures of holding violent criminals accountable for the crimes they commit. Does it make sense why Democrats want stricter gun restrictions for law-abiding citizens but fail to prosecute those carrying illegal firearms? How can any honest and objective person not question this? What about those who provide guns to known felons? Remember, the man who provided the gun to Officer French's killer was released on $4,500 in bail!

★ ★ ★

In 2012, the socialist government of Venezuela enacted the Control of Arms, Munitions and Disarmament Law with the objective of *disarming all* citizens. Before this new law was made, Venezuelan citizens with a gun permit were able purchase firearms; once the new law was enacted, all gun sales were prohibited except to government entities. Under the new law, the penalty for illegally carrying or selling a firearm is up to twenty years in prison.

So, did this new law reduce violence? No! In 2015, Venezuela had a population of just over thirty million people and 27,875 homicides—the highest rate in the *world.* The 2015 homicide total was up significantly from the 18,000-plus homicides in 2011 before the Control of Arms, Munitions and Disarmament Law was enacted. In comparison, the United States recorded 15,883 homicides in 2015 with a population of just over 320 million—a murder rate almost nineteen times lower than that of Venezuela. Restrictive gun laws do not deter criminals from obtaining and using firearms; they take them out of the hands of law-abiding citizens.

It should also be noted that the presidential administration pushing gun restrictions domestically allowed billions of dollars of US military equipment—paid for by *your* tax dollars—to fall into Taliban hands during their takeover of Afghanistan. It is believed the Taliban took possession of two thousand armored vehicles (including US Humvees), forty aircraft (potentially including UH-60 Black Hawks), scout attack helicopters, ScanEagle military drones as well as M4 rifles, M16 rifles, M24 sniper rifles, .50 caliber machine guns, night-vision goggles and radios. Between 2004 and 2016, the US gave the Afghan military almost 600,000 weapons and over 75,000 vehicles.

The withdrawal of US troops from Afghanistan and the subsequent takeover by the Taliban could not have been handled worse by the Biden Administration. After the embarrassment, Biden officials directed federal agencies to scrap their websites of official reports detailing the **$82.9 billion** in military equipment and training provided to the Afghan security forces dating back to 2001!

In this chapter, I used the data for intentional murders—referred to as murders, criminal homicides, or non-negligent homicides—for all the statistics. These numbers are different from total homicides, as homicides include murders as well as justified homicides. The murders are generally between 9 percent and 13 percent lower than the total homicide count. For example, Missouri had 738 murders and 803 total homicides, Tennessee had 699 murders and 753 total homicides, and Illinois had 1,166 murders and 1,343 total homicides. In many articles, the words "murders" and "homicides" are used interchangeably and incorrectly, as many journalists don't seem to understand the difference.

Chapter Eleven

Packing up, leaving your home and your job, and enrolling your kids in a new school aren't easy things to do, but oftentimes a major change is good or even necessary. Throughout history, countless Americans have migrated in search of greener pastures. This is no different today as we are witnessing many Americans say "I've had enough," pack up and leave what has been their home. There has been a slow but continuous migration out of liberal cities and states for decades that rapidly accelerated beginning in 2020. This substantial domestic migration in the first part of the 2020s has been quite evident, as millions of families are packing up and moving due to one or more of the very topics discussed in this book. Many domestic refugees are fleeing the destructive policies of blue states such as New York, Illinois, and California and heading to greener pastures in more conservative states, such as the Carolinas, Florida, Georgia, Texas, Utah, Idaho and Arizona.

Let's look at the states that lost and gained electoral votes (and US House seats) in the 2020 census.

States that Lost Electoral Votes in 2020

New York	Ohio
Illinois	Michigan
Pennsylvania	California
West Virginia	

States that Gained Electoral Votes in 2020

Texas (Gained 2)	Colorado
Florida	Oregon
North Carolina	Montana

As you can see, there was only a reorganization of seven electoral votes between the 2010 and 2020 censuses, with California losing its first ever. We will see a much larger shift in electoral votes in the 2030 census than we did in 2020, as the radical Progressive social issues being pushed by Democrats came to the forefront after the census responses were due in April of 2020. In conjunction with already higher taxes, these Progressive social issues—such as criminal justice reform and woke ideology in public schools in addition to the Covid restrictions in 2020 and 2021—exacerbated a mass exodus of people leaving the areas that have created these problems.

This migration will continue over the next several years and be evident in the 2030 census. California could very possibly lose four electoral votes this decade, along with New York losing three and Illinois two! New York City alone lost over three hundred thousand people from July 2020 to July 2021 with San Francisco, Chicago and Los Angeles all losing over forty thousand residents during the same time span. Philadelphia, Portland, San Jose, Baltimore, Boston, Minneapolis, Saint Paul and Washington, DC, also lost residents in 2020 and 2021. The exodus from these and other cities will continue as long as their residents keep electing Democrats!

Traditionally conservative-leaning states in the South and Mountain West will continue to gain more domestic refugees over the next several years. Texas and Florida are seeing a large number of new residents, which will likely result in Texas gaining as many as four electoral votes in 2030 and Florida as many as three. Utah, Idaho, Arizona, North Carolina, and Georgia will almost certainly gain one with the possibility for Tennessee, South Carolina and Nevada to gain as well. On the flip side, Pennsylvania will likely lose another electoral vote as well as Oregon losing the one it just picked up this past census. Other states that could have one less congressional representative in 2030 are Michigan, Rhode Island and Minnesota.

So, why is this important? Well, domestic refugees who arrive in their new, more conservative states often continue to vote in the same damaging way—which is why so many of them left in the first place. You would think they would learn, but many of them don't! In the 2020 presidential election, the traditionally and reliably red states of Georgia and Arizona flipped blue, accounting for a total of twenty-seven electoral votes. The same thing happened in the prior decade with the formerly red states of Virginia and Colorado, accounting for a total twenty-two electoral votes (at the time). Electoral votes decide presidents, and presidents nominate Supreme Court justices—the two most powerful bodies in the United States.

Domestic migration has been evident in the past several election cycles. Those who closely follow elections and population trends shouldn't be too surprised about the states of Georgia and Arizona going blue for the 2020 presidential ticket. The margins in these previously red states have become all the more narrow throughout the past decade.

Let's look at Georgia. In the 2012 presidential race, Republican Mitt Romney won the state by more than 300,000 votes over Democrat incumbent Barack Obama (2,078,688 to 1,773,827). In 2016, Donald

Trump defeated Democrat Hillary Clinton by over 200,000 votes (2,089,104 to 1,877,963). In a very high-turnout 2020 election, Joe Biden won the state, defeating Donald Trump by a razor-thin margin of around 10,000 votes (2,473,633 to 2,461,854).

Now, let's look at the Georgia governor races. In 2014, Republican incumbent Nathan Deal defeated Democrat Jason Carter by around 200,000 votes (1,345,237 to 1,144,794). Four years later it was a much closer election, as Republican Brian Kemp defeated Democrat Stacey Abrams by around 55,000 votes (1,978,408 to 1,923,685).

Georgia Presidential Elections (Past Decade)

	Republican Candidate Total Votes	Democratic Candidate Total Votes
2012:	2,070,221	1,761,761
2016:	2,068,623	1,837,300
2020:	2,461,854	2,473,633

Georgia Governor Elections (Past Decade)

	Republican Candidate Total Votes	Democratic Candidate Total Votes
2014:	1,341,161	1,138,476
2018:	1,978,408	1,923,685

There has been a huge push in the state of Georgia over the last several years to register young voters and Black voters—both of whom vote highly for Democrats. This, combined with blue state refugees, has shifted the electoral demographic in Georgia from red to purple. Ok, Trump supporters—can you start looking at the facts and focus on the 45th President's effective policies, *not* election fraud?!

A Major Cause for Concern

Americans who care about the future of the country should be concerned about the state of Texas having the same fate as that of Virginia, Colorado, Georgia and Arizona. In the 2012 presidential election, Romney defeated Obama by over 1,250,000 votes in Texas (4,569,843 to 3,308,124). Four years later, Trump defeated Clinton by over 800,000 votes (4,685,047 to 3,877,868). In 2020, Trump again won the state of Texas, this time by over 500,000 votes (5,890,347 to 5,259,126).

In 2012, Republican Ted Cruz defeated Democrat Paul Sadler by a very comfortable 4,440,137 to 3,194,927 margin for US Senator representing Texas. Six years later, when Cruz was running for re-election, he won by just over 200,000 votes, defeating Progressive Democrat Beto O'Rourke (4,260,553 to 4,045,632). Greg Abbott won election for governor of Texas by comfortable margins in both 2014 and 2018 and is facing O'Rourke in his 2022 re-election bid. In a likely "red wave" year, Abbott will probably win re-election by more than 750,000 votes (over ten points), but Texas is not the deep red state it was a decade ago.

Texas Presidential Elections

	Republican Candidate Total Votes	Democratic Candidate Total Votes
2012:	4,569,843	3,308,124
2016:	4,685,047	3,877,868
2020:	5,890,347	5,259,126

Texas Senator Elections

	Republican Candidate Total Votes	Democratic Candidate Total Votes
2012:	4,440,137	3,194,927
2018:	4,260,553	4,045,632

Factors such as national environment and candidate popularity influence elections but it is obvious that Texas as a whole has been trending to the left over the past decade. Why? Well, Texas has gained almost eight million new residents between 2000 and 2020 (thus six more Electoral College votes over this span), many of them from domestic migration. Data from the US Census Bureau says that more than 687,000 people have moved from California to Texas from 2010 to 2020. Texas has a solid job market, no state income tax, affordable real estate (relatively speaking), cheap gas, limited Covid restrictions in 2020 and 2021, and does not promote woke social policies on a state level as California does.

Texas gaining so many Democrat voters is very concerning for two reasons. First and most obvious are the forty electoral votes currently at stake, and second is oil! Texas is by far the top oil-producing state in the nation, producing a total of 1.78 billion barrels in the year 2020, which accounted for over 43 percent of all the oil produced in the US that year. The five states that produced the next highest shares in 2020 were North Dakota, New Mexico, Oklahoma, Colorado and Alaska. These five states accounted for a combined total of 31.69 percent of all domestic oil produced in that year—over 11 percent *less* than Texas produced by itself! Gulf of Mexico waters are under federal jurisdiction and accounted for 14.6 percent of US oil production in 2020.

After the 2010 midterm election, Texas had a total of 19 Republican and 12 Democratic State Senators and 101 Republicans and 49 Democrats in the Texas State House. After the 2020 general election, there were a total of 18 Republican and 13 Democratic State Senators and 85 Republicans and 64 Democrats in the State House. If Democrats gain control of the Texas State Legislature or governor's office before we have alternate energy sources ready for use nationwide, not only Texas but *all* states will be in deep trouble. We saw what happened to the price of oil in 2021 and 2022 when production didn't meet the demand of the consumers…

Imagine if Beto O'Rourke gets elected as governor of Texas in 2026 and writes an executive order stopping or greatly limiting drilling, or if the Texas State Legislature passes a large tax on each barrel of oil produced. Given the huge share of the marketplace Texas has on oil, what do you think would happen to the price if production there is strangled? If you think gas prices have been high in 2022, you better hope Democrats don't take control of Texas in the next several years! The fate of Texas could possibly lean on the shoulders of the state's Hispanic voters. If Hispanic voters continue to shift to the right, Texas will likely remain a red-leaning state; if not, it might very possibly be a pure toss-up by the end of this decade.

★ ★ ★

California is a very beautiful state with a temperate climate, but it has become undesirable to millions and millions of people. In addition to the very high cost of real estate and general living, Californians are fed up with the insane curriculum being introduced in public schools, the increased homeless population, increased crime due to criminals not being prosecuted, dirty streets, and fear of big government.

No city in the US is losing a higher percentage of its residents than San Francisco. From April 2020 to July 2021, San Francisco lost almost *sixty thousand* residents, or an astonishing 7 percent of the city's total population! The outbound exodus will continue. Many recent polls have found that close to half of the city's residents plan to leave in the next few years. San Francisco has been a liberal city with a high cost of living for decades, but it continued to increase in population until 2020. The pandemic and the increased option of remote work had an impact on the outward migration, but this was more of an opportunity for people to leave rather than the main reason they left.

Most residents in the polls are blaming homelessness and crime. Assaults, thefts, car break-ins, defecation, and open-air narcotics abuse and dealing are out of control—70 percent of residents in one poll feel the quality of life has declined in the city, 80 percent say crime has worsened in recent years and 88 percent say homelessness has worsened. Even the reported incidents of human or animal feces have more than doubled in the past several years, as shown below.

Total Incidents of Reported Feces in San Francisco by Year

2015:	13,346	2018:	28,313
2016:	18,544	2019:	30,894
2017:	20,895	2020:	28,240

Who wants to go have a Sunday lunch in San Francisco and see feces, trash or dirty needles in the street? Any takers?

Population of San Francisco

1990:	723,959	2020:	873,965
2000:	776,733	2021:	815,201
2010:	805,235		

The state of California is in major trouble, but the people running the state keep governing based on ideology rather than admitting their policies might not work and attempting to change them. Thus, the only way to change the quality of life will be to vote for more reasonable candidates.

In 2019, the three states receiving the most former Californians were Texas, Arizona and Nevada, receiving 82,235, 59,713 and 47,322 respectively. Roughly one million people left California for other states in 2020 and 2021—almost 650,000 in 2020 and over 360,000 in 2021! One would think the hordes of Californians leaving the state would vote against such destructive policies in their new states, but often, they don't.

THE GOOD NEWS

Don't get too discouraged! Population trends and voting trends change over time. Just look at the Electoral College map of, say, the 1976 presidential election. While many states in the South have been shifting to the left, those in the Midwest are going the opposite direction. We saw this in Trump's 2016 presidential victory, as he won not only Ohio and Iowa but also Pennsylvania, Michigan and Wisconsin—a total of 67 electoral votes! It's not surprising that Ohio and Iowa have become safe red states, nor will it be a surprise to see Wisconsin and Pennsylvania as likely red states.

Another interesting state to look at is Illinois. Yes, Illinois—ok, call me insane! If you don't think the currently blue state of Illinois can change, you may be surprised. The majority of Illinois is conservative-leaning, but highly liberal/Progressive Cook County makes up 40 percent of the state's population and controls much of the state's politics. Cook County as a whole lost residents from the 2010 to the 2020 census. Could we see the population of the Windy City shrink more and more until it loses its stranglehold on the state's politics? Given the high crime, cold weather and terrible leadership Chicago has, it is possible.

Chicago won't lose an astonishing 65 percent of its population as Detroit has, but could Cook County lose 400,000 voters over the next decade? Yes, it could! In the 2018 governor election, Pritzker defeated Republican Bruce Rauner 2,479,746 to 1,765,751—a relatively wide margin. This margin isn't nearly as significant, however, when you factor in 192,527 third-party votes for Conservative Party candidate Sam McCann and 109,518 for Libertarian Party candidate Grayson Jackson. In the 2020 presidential election, Trump had a total of 142,680 votes more than Biden in the 101 combined Illinois counties not named Cook.

Given rural America's dislike for the current Democratic Party, downstate Illinois will only become a deeper shade of red in the foreseeable future. The future of Illinois statewide elections, however, depends on the suburbs. If suburban counties surrounding Chicago such as DuPage, Will and Kane get tired of the high property taxes, as well as the outrageous crime and poor leadership in neighboring Chicago and start voting to the right, there are enough votes to swing statewide elections and, of course, win the local ones.

I'm not saying Illinois will become a red state; I'm saying that, like its Midwestern neighbors, it will trend to the right. It wouldn't be surprising to see Illinois as a lean-blue state (rather than a deep blue state) by the end of this decade. A survey by Morning Consult done in the first quarter of 2022 found that Biden's net approval rating among registered voters in Illinois is only a positive 2 percent—17 percent less than his approval rate among California voters! Hang in there, Illinois friends!

OTHER BRIGHT SPOTS

Another sunny spot, in a partly to mostly cloudy forecast, is the Sunshine State. As domestic migrants search for greener pastures, Florida fortunately is not following the same leftward trend as many other states in the South. Florida and its 30 electoral votes is, in fact, trending to the right. One major factor is the demographic of its residents. As a whole, older voters vote to the right of their younger counterparts, and Florida has the fifth highest median age in the nation at 42.7 years. In contrast, the median age of Texans is 35.2 years. Another difference is that Florida's Hispanic voters vote more conservatively than Hispanic voters nationwide. As discussed in chapter five, Florida has a large population of Cuban voters, many of whom are familiar with the Communist regime that has controlled Cuba, and thus they wisely vote against the dangers of big government!

Ron DeSantis has done a tremendous job in the state of Florida.

He has been incredibly successful in fighting for parental rights, small businesses, supporting law enforcement and even fighting for (and drawing) a fair electoral college map in his state. The dishonest media accused DeSantis of gerrymandering and drawing a racist map, both of which are completely untrue accusations. Just so you can see for yourselves, the new map drawn by DeSantis in 2020 and the prior map drawn after the last census in 2010 are included below. Also included for comparison is Illinois' electoral map.

Current Electoral College Map of Florida (2022–2030 Elections)

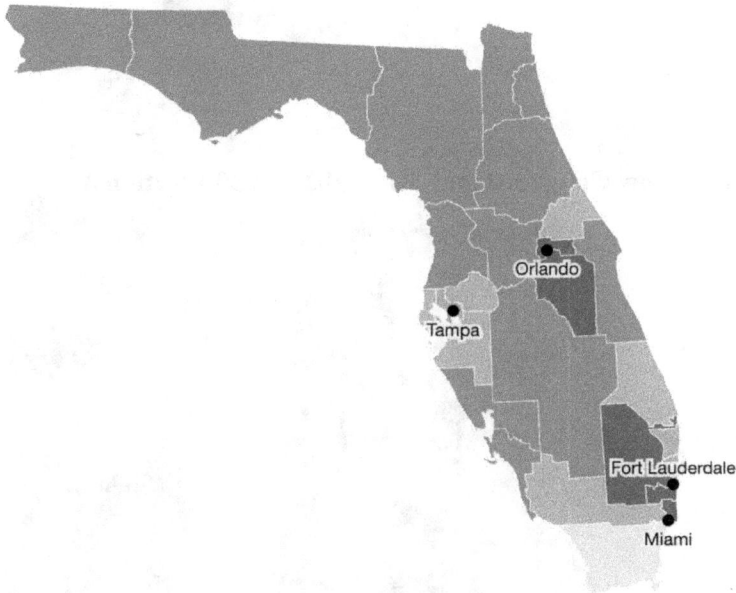

Previous Electoral College Map of Florida (2012–2020 Elections)

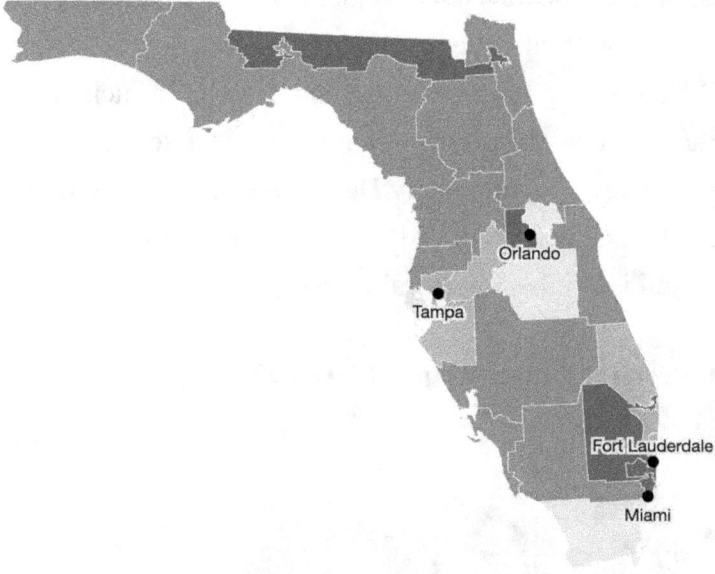

Illinois' New Congressional Map (2022–2030 Elections)

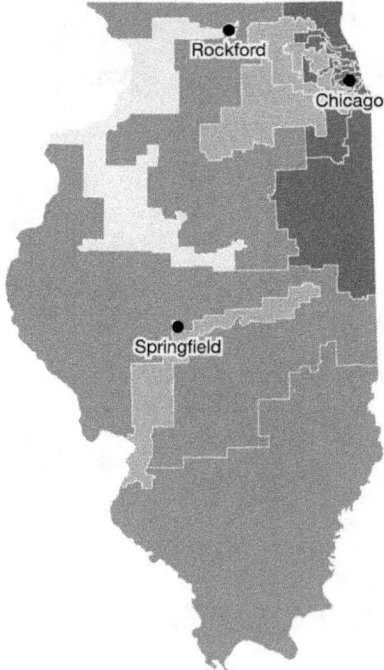

**Close Up Map of US House Districts
in the Chicagoland Area**

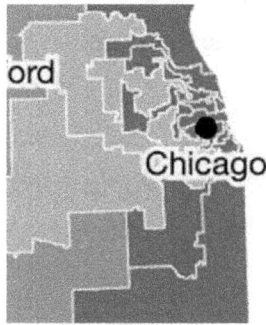

Ok, which state has the gerrymandered electoral map again? You decide...

What has the media said about this bogus Illinois map?

Congressional maps are redrawn every decade after the census and used for the election cycles for the rest of that decade.

**There are 435 US electoral districts and one representative is elected per district. These 435 persons make up the members of the US House of Representatives, and they, in addition to the 100 US Senators, account for the 535 Electoral College members and votes. The Electoral College districts are based on population. When electing a president, it's a "winner takes all" system in forty-eight states, meaning the candidate who wins the popular vote in those states takes all of the electoral votes. **

★ ★ ★

One last positive to mention is the Senate forecast. It appears there will be a few tight races in the 2022 midterms that will decide who controls the Senate for the next two years. I predict that Republicans will win in Florida, North Carolina, Ohio, Nevada and Wisconsin by more comfortable margins than most people think. Winning these states will give the Republicans fifty seats in the Senate.

The races in Arizona, New Hampshire, and Pennsylvania look like they will be close. I expect between these three and the much talked about state of Georgia, the Republicans will end up taking back the majority. One of the most accurate pollsters in recent elections, Trafalgar Group, even has a close Senate race in Washington State, but I'm not going to get my hopes up for that one. There are several Senate seats currently held by Democrats that are up for re-election in 2024 that Republicans should flip, allowing them to comfortably hold the Senate for the rest of this decade. The GOP should be able to keep this margin for some time to come!

Trafalgar Group was overall less accurate in 2022 than they had been in the preceding elections. They overestimated the Republican candidates in many races.

Final Thoughts

Over the next few decades, I fear, America will continue its slide to the left. How far, we don't know. The left has tremendous assistance from most of the media, many school boards, and many departments of education across the country, and they have been successful in dividing Americans by many categories such as wealth, race, and sexual orientation. The virtue signaling has fooled millions, and many Republicans have unfortunately played into that hand.

Entitlement programs have been successful in recruiting voters, many of whom don't understand the bigger picture, and the immense inflation has led more and more to believe assistance from the government is necessary to survive. The massive amounts of violent crime won't slow down, as police departments will continue to struggle with staffing, particularly those in areas controlled by the Progressive left as the lawmakers there make law enforcement careers less and less desirable. The leftist district attorneys and judges will continue to stick with their partisan narrative of releasing violent criminals rather than giving merit to the crime stats or doing what's right for the victims. Leftist politicians will keep proposing, passing and supporting laws that help the offenders, hurt the victims and peace officers, and tie the hands of those district attorneys and judges who want to keep violent offenders off the streets. Of course, these same politicians will keep their own security beefed up. Certain aspects of society will get worse and more people will have less, but we will adjust! Americans will continue to seek and find greener pastures as we have throughout history.

The truth is that capitalism and socialism are both evil. Businesses and the government both want us in debt to them because it takes away our power and adds to theirs. We live in a cruel world, but in the midst of it most people just want simple lives. The best way to live our simple lives is by having freedom. Democrats give us the worst chance to have this.

Even in this cruel world, life is beautiful. We owe it to ourselves to enjoy our freedoms every day! Make sure they last!

Author's Note

The majority of this book is based on facts, but some predictions were made. Any predictions or opinions, however, were made from the facts. I generally included quotes from both sides of the spectrum when presenting an issue, a basic standard that much of the media no longer practices. I did my best to get information from the primary source, or the closest possible source to that. For example, if I quoted the president, I went to statements and releases from the White House rather than a news outlet. When I wrote about a bill, I got the text directly from the actual bill rather than from the aforementioned news outlet. I did not include any information I could not confirm from at least two sources.

There was no new content added after October of 2022. Like a large number of people who closely followed the 2022 elections, I overestimated how the Republican candidates would do overall. The prediction relating to the number of Republicans who would hold Senate seats after the 2022 election was thus off. Other predictions, such as my discussions about the state of Florida and the success DeSantis has had there, fared much better. Time will tell on other predictions, such as what the 2030 Electoral College map will look like.

In recent history, financial issues such as high inflation, high gas prices, a housing crisis or a poor-performing stock market have swung elections, but 2022 was different, as it seems the social issues were of equal or greater importance for many voters. I guess I shouldn't be surprised, given the social issues were what drove me to write this book. These issues are more divisive for the American people and are deep core issues that cannot be underestimated in future elections.

Sources

Chapter 1

1. Kate Hardiman – University of Notre Dame, "Most college students think America invented slavery, professor finds." The College Fix, October 31, 2016, Most college students think America invented slavery, professor finds | The College Fix.

2. "Code of Hammurabi." History.com, November 9, 2009, updated February 21, 2020, Code of Hammurabi: Laws & Facts – HISTORY.

3. Tom Lindsay, "After All, Didn't America Invent Slavery?" Forbes, August 30, 2019, https://www.forbes.com/sites/tomlindsay/2019/08/30/after-all-didnt-america-invent-slavery/.

4. "Philosophers justifying slavery." BBC, BBC - Ethics - Slavery: Philosophers justifying slavery.

5. "When Europeans Were Slaves: Research Suggests White Slavery Was Much More Common Than Previously Believed," Ohio State News – osu.edu, March 07, 2004, Research Suggests White Slavery Was Much More Common (osu.edu).

6. Thomas Lewis, "transatlantic slave trade." Britannica, August 23, 2022, Transatlantic slave trade | History & Facts | Britannica.

7. Michael Guasco, "The Misguided Focus on 1619 as the Beginning of Slavery in the U.S. Damages Our Understanding of American History." Smithsonian Magazine, September 13, 2017, The Misguided Focus on 1619 as the Beginning of Slavery in the U.S. Damages Our Understanding of American History | History| Smithsonian Magazine.

Chapter 2

1. Anthony Iaccarino, "The Founding Fathers and Slavery." Britannica, The Founding Fathers and Slavery | Britannica.

2. "Benjamin Franklin's Anti-Slavery Petitions to Congress." National Archives – The Center for Legislative Archives, Benjamin Franklin's Anti-Slavery Petitions to Congress | National Archives.

3. "Amistad Case." History.com, October 27, 2009, updated September 23, 2019, Amistad Case - Date, Facts & Significance - HISTORY.

4. "The Dred Scott Decision." U.S. History, The Dred Scott Decision [ushistory. org].

5. "Dred Scott v. Sandford." Wikipedia, Dred Scott v. Sandford - Wikipedia.

Chapter 3

1. Helen Miller Bailey, *40 American Biographies*, California State Department of Education, Published 1967.

2. Rebecca Beatrice Brooks, "The Life of Harriet Tubman." Civil War Saga, August 19, 2011, The Life of Harriet Tubman - CIVIL WAR SAGA.

3. "Harriet Tubman." History.com, October 29, 2009, updated January 26, 2022, Harriet Tubman: Facts, Underground Railroad & Legacy - HISTORY.

4. Renee Ater, "NY State Network to Freedom: William Seward and Harriet Tubman Statue." Schenectady, October 13, 2019, NY State Network to Freedom: William Seward and Harriet Tubman Statue, Schenectady — Renée Ater (reneeater.com).

5. Russell Freedman, *Lincoln: A Photobiography*. Clarion Books, Published 1987.

6. "Civil War Casualties." HistoryNet, Civil War Casualties (historynet.com).

7. "Black Soldiers in the U.S. Military During the Civil War." National Archives – Educator Resources, Black Soldiers in the U.S. Military During the Civil War | National Archives.

Chapter 4

1. "Censorship in the Empire of Japan." Wikipedia, Censorship in the Empire of Japan - Wikipedia.

2. "Nanjing Massacre." History.com, November 9, 2009, updated June 7, 2019, Rape of Nanjing: Massacre, Definition & Aftermath - HISTORY - HISTORY.

3. Primus V., "Lessons in Surprise." Harvard Magazine, July–August 2010, Yamamoto at Harvard, and a Harvard Community Garden | Harvard Magazine.

4. "Operation Vengeance: The Killing of Isoroku Yamamoto." The National WWII Museum- New Orleans, April 26, 2023. Operation Vengeance: The Killing of Isoroku Yamamoto | The National WWII Museum | New Orleans (nationalw-w2museum.org).

5. Morgan Phillips, "Ilhan Omar calls for dismantling America's 'system of oppression.'" Fox News, July 7, 2020, Ilhan Omar calls for dismantling America's 'system of oppression' | Fox News.

6. "Ilhan Omar." Biography, April 13, 2021, Ilhan Omar - Politics, Husband & Facts - Biography.

7. Mark Moore, "Rep. Omar has paid husband's political consulting firm nearly $2.8M." New York Post, November 11, 2020, Rep. Omar paid husband's consulting firm nearly $2.8M since 2019: report (nypost.com).

8. Jorge Fitz-Gibbon, "Rep. Omar's campaign reportedly funded 80 percent of her husband's consulting firm." New York Post, February 7, 2021, Ilhan Omar's campaign funded her husband's consulting firm: report (nypost.com).

9. "Rep. Omar terminates contract with husband's consulting firm." AP News, November 16, 2020, Rep. Omar terminates contract with husband's consulting firm | AP News.

10. David Smurthwaite, *The Pacific War Atlas 1941–1945*. Mirabel Books Ltd., Published 1995.

11. Ray C. Hunt & Bernard Norling, *Behind Japanese Lines*. The University Press of Kentucky, Copyright 1986.

12. "Fla. Governor Ron DeSantis says he wants to stop 'huge problem' of Chinese investors purchasing US real estate." Nextshark – on Yahoo.com, Jane Nam, July 25, 2022, Fla. Governor Ron DeSantis says he wants to stop 'huge problem' of Chinese investors purchasing US real estate (yahoo.com).

13. Ariel Zilber, "Ron DeSantis blasts China for buying up US farmland: 'It's a huge problem.'" New York Post, July 25, 2022, Ron DeSantis blasts China for buying up Florida farmland (nypost.com).

14. "What You Should Know About Buying Property in China as a Foreigner." YK Law, Buying Property in China as a Foreigner | YK Law.

15. By Mark Oliver, Checked by Leah Silverman, "Inside the Pacific Theater: The World War II Horror Show History Wants To Forget." ATI, August 6, 2019, updated September 22, 2021, Inside The Pacific War, The Most Horrifying Theater In WW2 (allthatsinteresting.com).

16. "Japanese war camps highlight 'lost' history through art." University of Canterbury, September 8, 2020, Japanese war camps highlight 'lost' history through art | University of Canterbury.

17. Ruben P. Kitchen, Jr., *Pacific Carrier*. Kensington Publishing Corp., 1980.

18. National D-Day Memorial. "Combat Medics of WWII," Combat Medics of WWII — Google Arts & Culture.

19. "Corpsman Up!" National Museum of the United States Navy, Corpsman Up! (navy.mil).

20. Seth Paltzer, "The Other Foe: The U.S. Army's Fight against Malaria in the Pacific Theater, 1942-45." The National Museum of the United States Army, The Other Foe: The U.S. Army's Fight against Malaria in the Pacific Theater, 1942-45 – The Campaign for the National Museum of the United States Army (armyhistory.org).

21. Grady Gallant, *The Friendly Dead*. Kensington Publishing Company, 1981.

22. Don Brown with Captain Jerry Yellin, *The Last Fighter Pilot*. Regnery Publishing, 2017.

23. Blake Stilwell, "The Story Behind the Two Flag Raisings at the Battle of Iwo Jima." Military.com, The Story Behind the Two Flag Raisings at the Battle of Iwo Jima | Military.com.

24. Office of U.S. Marine Corps Communication, Headquarters Marine Corps, "USMC Statement on Iwo Jima Flag Raisers." Marines, June 23, 2016, USMC statement on Iwo Jima flag raisers > United States Marine Corps Flagship > News Display (marines.mil).

25. "The Battle for Iwo Jima." The National WWII Museum – New Orleans, Iwo Jima Fact Sheet (nationalww2museum.org).

26. Linda Sieg, "Historians battle over Okinawa WW2 mass suicides." Reuters, April 6, 2007, Historians battle over Okinawa WW2 mass suicides | Reuters.

27. "Conversation on the Manhattan Project and Secrecy – From Henry Stimson, Secretary of War, To Harry S. Truman, Senator, Date: June 17, 1943." NuclearFiles.org, Nuclear Files: Library: Correspondence: Harry S. Truman: Conversation, July 17, 1943.

28. "The Kyujo Conspiracy – How a Group of Japanese Officers Planned to Overthrow the Emperor and Continue WW2." Military History Now, August 1, 2016, The Kyūjō Conspiracy – How a Group of Japanese Officers Planned to Overthrow the Emperor and Continue WW2 - MilitaryHistoryNow.com.

29. Donald J. Kinney, *Slambang 69*. Copyright 2003.

30. "Occupation of Japan and the New Constitution." PBS, Occupation of Japan and the New Constitution | American Experience | Official Site | PBS.

31. "Occupation of Japan (1945–1952) Primary Resources." MacArthur Memorial Education Programs, Occupation-of-Japan-Primary-Resources (macarthurmemorial.org).

32. Kanoko Matsuyama, "Japan Leads the G-7 in Covid Shots Without a Mandate in Sight." Bloomberg, November 16, 2021, Japan Leads the G-7 in Covid Shots Without a Mandate in Sight - Bloomberg.

Chapter 5

1. "Korean War." History.com, Korean War - Causes, Timeline & Veterans - HISTORY.

2. "GDP Ranked by Country 2022." World Population Review, GDP Ranked by Country 2022 (worldpopulationreview.com).

3. Prableen Bajpai, Reviewed by Julius Mansa, Fact- checked by Yarilet Perez, "North Korean vs. South Korean Economies: What's the Difference?" Investopedia, Updated December 31, 2021, Understanding North Korean vs. South Korean Economies (investopedia.com).

4. Bethaney Phillips, "These are the subtle differences between North and South Korea." We Are The Mighty, November 2, 2021, These are the subtle differences between North and South Korea (wearethemighty.com).

5. Talia Lakritz, "The leaders of North and South Korea met for the first time in 11 years – see the shocking difference between life in the 2 countries." Insider, April 27, 2018, PHOTOS: the Difference Between North and South Korea (insider.com).

6. "Pre-Castro Cuba." PBS, Pre-Castro Cuba | American Experience | Official Site | PBS.

7. Reuters Staff, "FACTBOX: Cuba's one-party political system." Reuters, February 22, 2008, FACTBOX: Cuba's one-party political system | Reuters.

8. Fred Lucas, "Cuban Americans Tell What Life Under Castro Was Really Like." The Daily Signal, February 24, 2020, Cuban Americans Tell What Life Under Castro Was Really Like (dailysignal.com).

9. "25 Things I Learned About Life in Cuba (after 53 Years of Fidel Castro rule)." Sher She Goes, 25 Things I Learned About Life in Cuba (after 53 Years of Fidel Castro rule) (shershegoes.com).

10. Jeff Desjardins, "Venezuela was once twelve times richer than China. What happened?" World Economic Forum, September 20, 2017, Venezuela was once twelve times richer than China. What happened? | World Economic Forum (weforum.org).

11. Maxim Lott, "How socialism turned Venezuela from the wealthiest country in South America into an economic basket case." Fox News, January 26, 2019, How socialism turned Venezuela from the wealthiest country in South America into an economic basket case | Fox News.

12. "Venezuela: Chavez Allies Pack Supreme Court." Human Rights Watch, December 13, 2004, Venezuela: Chávez Allies Pack Supreme Court | Human Rights Watch (hrw.org).

13. Seana Davis, Emmanuelle Saliba, and Alex Morgan, "Venezuela: 1 litre of milk could cost a third of your wage." Euronews, July 26, 2019, Venezuela: 1 litre of milk could cost a third of your wage | #TheCube | Euronews.

14. "Venezuela crisis: How the political situation escalated." BBC, August 12, 2021, Venezuela crisis: How the political situation escalated - BBC News.

15. David Kopel and Vincent Harinam, "In the wake of a gun ban, Venezuela sees rising homicide rate." The Hill, 4/19/18, In the wake of a gun ban, Venezuela sees rising homicide rate | The Hill.

16. "Venezuela bans private gun ownership." BBC, June 1, 2012, Venezuela bans private gun ownership - BBC News.

17. Sabrina Rodriguez and Matt Dixon, "Biden's Cuba and Venezuela policy shifts leave Florida Democrats dismayed." Politico, 5/18/22, Biden's Cuba and Venezuela policy shifts leave Florida Democrats dismayed - POLITICO.

18. Jens Manuel Krogstad, "Most Cuban American voters identify as Republican in 2020." Pew Research Center, October 2, 2020, Most Cuban American voters identify as Republican in 2020 | Pew Research Center.

19. Maria Isabel Puerta Riera, "Magazuelans: How Venezuelan Americans Embraced Trump as Their Savior." NACLA, January 15, 2021, Magazuelans: How Venezuelan Americans Embraced Trump as Their Savior | NACLA.

20. Carmen Sesin, "Trump cultivated the Latino vote in Florida, and it paid off." NBC News, November 3, 2020, Trump cultivated the Latino vote in Florida, and it paid off (nbcnews.com).

21. Holly K. Sonneland, "Chart How U.S. Latinos Voted in the 2020 Presidential Election." AS/COA, November 5, 2020, Chart: How U.S. Latinos Voted in the 2020 Presidential Election | AS/COA (as-coa.org).

22. Election Results Archive, Miami-Dade County: 2020 General Election and 2016 General Election, Election Results Archive (miamidade.gov).

23. "Governor Ron DeSantis Holds Roundtable to Support the Cuban People." July 13, 2021, Governor Ron DeSantis Holds Roundtable to Support the Cuban People (flgov.com).

24. Marc Frank and Mario Fuentes, "In Cuba's poorest neighborhoods, youths could face decades in jail after protests." Reuters, January 14, 2022, In Cuba's poorest neighborhoods, youths could face decades in jail after protests | Reuters.

25. Reuters, "U.S. sends 119 Cuban migrants home as growing number take to sea." NBC News, January 5, 2022, U.S. sends 119 Cuban migrants home as growing number take to sea (nbcnews.com).

26. "Secretary Mayorkas Overviews U.S. Maritime Migrant Interdiction Operations." U.S. Department of Homeland Security, July 13, 2021, Secretary

Mayorkas Overviews U.S. Maritime Migrant Interdiction Operations | Homeland Security (dhs.gov).

27. "Southwest Land Border Encounters." U.S. Customs and Border Protection, Last modified October 13, 2022, Southwest Land Border Encounters | U.S. Customs and Border Protection (cbp.gov).

28. Melissa Holzberg, "From 'Bonehead Idea' To Studying It: Joe Biden's Shifting Positions on Court Packing." Forbes, April 15, 2021, From 'Bonehead Idea' To Studying It: Joe Biden's Shifting Positions On Court Packing (forbes.com).

29. "President Biden to Sign Executive Order Creating the Presidential Commission on the Supreme Court of the United States." The White House, April 9, 2021, President Biden to Sign Executive Order Creating the Presidential Commission on the Supreme Court of the United States | The White House.

Chapter 6

1. Mike Cummings, "Covid school closures most harm students from poorest neighborhoods." YaleNews, January 5, 2021, COVID school closures most harm students from poorest neighborhoods | YaleNews.

2. K. Winters, "Do as I say: California governor sends his children back to a wealthy private school while public schools remain closed." Law Enforcement Today, November 2, 2020, Gavin Newsom sends his children back to a wealthy private school (lawenforcementtoday.com).

3. Amy Graff, "California Gov. Newsom's 4 kids are back in the classroom at private school." SFGATE, November 2, 2020, California Gov. Newsom's 4 kids are back in the classroom at private school (sfgate.com).

4. Hannah Poukish and Alex Cohen, "Los Angeles Loses Most Small Businesses in the US Since Pandemic Began." Spectrum News 1, February 5, 2021, Los Angeles Loses Most Small Businesses in the US (spectrumnews1.com).

5. Bill Melugin and Shelly Insheiwat, "Fox 11 obtains exclusive photos of Gov. Newsom at French restaurant allegedly not following COVID-19 protocols." Fox 11 Los Angeles, November 17, 2020, FOX 11 obtains exclusive photos of Gov. Newsom at French restaurant allegedly not following COVID-19 protocols (foxla.com).

6. Sydney Kalich and Shahan Ahmed, "Gov. Newsom Declares State of Emergency in LA on Fourth Day of Protests." NBC4, May 30, 2020, updated May 31, 2020, Gov. Newsom Declares State of Emergency in LA on Fourth Day of Protests – NBC Los Angeles.

7. Bill Hutchinson, "Federal court backs California Gov. Gavin Newsom's orders keeping churches closed." ABC News, May 24, 2020, Federal court backs California Gov. Gavin Newsom's orders keeping churches closed - ABC News.

8. Bruce Haring, "US Supreme Court Lifts Ban On Indoor Church Services In California." Deadline, February 6, 2021, US Supreme Court Lifts Ban On Indoor Church Services In California – Deadline.

9. "Explaining Operation Warp Speed." USA Department of Health and Human Services/United States of America Department of Defense, Explaining Operation Warp Speed (nihb.org).

10. Paul Roderick Gregory, "Getting the facts right on Operation Warp Speed." The Hill, March 20, 2021, Getting the facts right on Operation Warp Speed | The Hill.

11. Caroline Kelly, "'I will not take his word for it': Kamala Harris says she would not trust Trump alone on a coronavirus vaccine." CNN. September 5, 2020, Kamala Harris says she would not trust President Donald Trump alone on a coronavirus vaccine | CNN Politics.

12. "Executive Order on Requiring Coronavirus Disease 2019 Vaccination for Federal Employees." The White House, September 9, 2021, Executive Order on Requiring Coronavirus Disease 2019 Vaccination for Federal Employees | The White House.

13. ArentFox Schiff, "Biden Announces Vaccine Mandates For Large Employers, Federal Employees and Contractors, and Health Care Employers." JDSupra, September 13, 2021, Biden Announces Vaccine Mandates For Large Employers, Federal Employees and Contractors, and Health Care Employers | ArentFox Schiff - JDSupra.

14. "National Federation of Independent Business v. Department of Labor, Occupational Safety and Health Administration." Supreme Court of the United States, January 13, 2022, 21A244 National Federation of Independent Business v. OSHA (01/13/2022) (supremecourt.gov).

15. "Statement by President Joe Biden On the U.S. Supreme Court's Decision on Vaccine Requirements." The White House, January 13, 2022, Statement by President Joe Biden On the U.S. Supreme Court's Decision on Vaccine Requirements | The White House.

16. "Tracking Coronavirus in Florida: Latest Map and Case Count." The New York Times, Florida Coronavirus Map and Case Count - The New York Times (nytimes.com).

17. "Tracking Coronavirus in New York: Latest Map and Case Count." The New York Times, New York Coronavirus Map and Case Count - The New York Times (nytimes.com).

18. "Tracking Coronavirus in Illinois: Latest Map and Case Count." The New York Times, Illinois Coronavirus Map and Case Count - The New York Times (nytimes.com).

19. "History of 1918 Flu Pandemic." CDC (Centers for Disease Control and Prevention), Last reviewed March 21, 2018, History of 1918 Flu Pandemic | Pandemic Influenza (Flu) | CDC.

20. Mason Bissada, "California Lawmaker Introduces Plan To Pay For State Universal Healthcare System." Forbes, January 6, 2022, California Lawmaker Introduces Plan To Pay For State Universal Healthcare System (forbes.com).

21. Dawn Allcot, "Legislative Win Could Lead to Government-Funded Healthcare in California by 2024." GoBankingRates.com – posted on Yahoo, January 20, 2022, Legislative Win Could Lead to Government-Funded Healthcare in California by 2024 (yahoo.com).

22. "California Home Values." Zillow, California Home Prices & Home Values | Zillow.

23. "California Mortgage Calculator: Estimate Your Monthly Payment." Money Geek, Last updated May 3, 2022, California Mortgage Calculator - Calculate Your Monthly Payment | MoneyGeek.com.

24. "Gas Prices." AAA, AAA Gas Prices.

25. Josh Gerstein and Alexander Ward, "Supreme Court has voted to overturn abortion rights, draft opinion shows." Politico, May 2, 2022, Updated May 3, 2022, Supreme Court has voted to overturn abortion rights, draft opinion shows - POLITICO.

26. Ben Feuerherd and Gabrielle Fonrouge, "Armed man Nicholas Roske arrested near Supreme Court Justice Brett Kavanaugh's home." New York Post, June 8, 2022, Nicholas Roske arrested with weapon near Brett Kavanaugh's home (nypost.com).

27. Dan Mangan and Kevin Breuninger, "Armed man who wanted to kill Supreme Court Justice Brett Kavanaugh told police he was upset over abortion, Uvalde." CNBC, June 8, 2022, Supreme Court: Armed man arrested near Brett Kavanaugh home (cnbc.com).

28. Ruth Sent Us, Ruth Sent Us.

29. Arjun Singh, "Pro-Abortion Group 'Ruth Sent Us' Suggests Targeting Amy Coney Barrett's Children." National Review, June 10, 2022, Ruth Sent Us: Target Amy Coney Barrett's Kids | National Review.

30. Jeff Diament and Besheer Mohamed, "What the data says about abortion in the U.S.," Pew Research Center, June 24, 2022, Abortion in the U.S.: What the data says | Pew Research Center.

31. Luu Ireland, MD, "Who are the 1 in 4 American women who choose abortion?" UMass Chan Medical School, May 30, 2019, Who are the 1 in 4 American women who choose abortion? (umassmed.edu).

Chapter 7

1. "Office of the Governor." State of California, October 08, 2021, CAP14-20211008124819.

2. "ESMC Glossary and Bibliography." California Department of Education, May 16, 2019, https://www.cde.ca.gov/be/cc/cd/documents/esmcglossarybibliography.docx.

3. "Income Inequality by State 2022." World Population Review, Income Inequality by State 2022 (worldpopulationreview.com).

4. Adam McCann, "Best States for Racial Equality in Education." WalletHub, June 7, 2022, Best States for Racial Equality in Education (wallethub.com).

5. Valerie Wilson, "Racial disparities in income and poverty remain largely unchanged amid strong income growth in 2019." Economic Policy Institute, September 16, 2020, Racial disparities in income and poverty remain largely unchanged amid strong income growth in 2019 | Economic Policy Institute (epi.org).

6. "Census Bureau Releases New Educational Attainment Data." United States Census Bureau, February 24, 2022, Census Bureau Releases New Educational Attainment Data.

7. Roger Clegg, "Percentage of Births to Unmarried Women." Center for Equal Opportunity, February 26, 2020, Percentage of Births to Unmarried Women | Center for Equal Opportunity (ceousa.org).

8. "Effects of Out-of-Wedlock Birth on Children." Marripedia, Effects of Out-of-Wedlock Birth on Children [Marripedia].

9. Devin Foley, "Chicago: 3 out of 4 Blacks Born out of Wedlock." Intellectual Takeout, January 9, 2017, Chicago: 3 out of 4 Blacks Born out of Wedlock - Intellectual Takeout.

10. Whet Moser, "Race, College, and College Completion in Chicago." Chicago Magazine, February 20, 2013, Race, College, and College Completion in Chicago – Chicago Magazine.

11. "Chicago City Council." Wikipedia, Chicago City Council - Wikipedia.

12. Trevor Bach, "The 10 U.S. Cities With the Largest Income Inequality Gaps." U.S. News, September 21, 2020. U.S. Cities With the Biggest Income Inequality Gaps (usnews.com).

13. "Black Lives Matter: What We Believe." black-Lives-Matter-Handout.pdf (uca. edu)

14. "Millionaire Statistics." Balancing Everything, 12/31/2021, Millionaire Statistics for 2022 | Balancing Everything.

15. Richard V. Reeves and Ember Smith, "The male college crisis is not just in enrollment, but completion." Brookings, October 8, 2021, The male college crisis is not just in enrollment, but completion (brookings.edu).

16. WTVR CBS 6 Web Staff, "Full transcription of Virginia's first gubernatorial debate." 6 News Richmond, September 16, 2021, Updated September 17, 2021, Full transcription of Virginia's first gubernatorial debate (wtvr.com).

17. Ned Oliver, Kate Masters, Graham Moomaw and Sarah Vogelsong, "Cheat sheet: Youngkin and McAuliffe on the issues." Virginia Mercury, November 1, 2021, Cheat sheet: Youngkin and McAuliffe on the issues - Virginia Mercury.

18. Moriah Balingit, "Va. governor vetoes charter school and 'Beloved' bills." The Washington Post, March 24, 2017, Va. governor vetoes charter school and 'Beloved' bills - The Washington Post.

19. Drew Wilder, "Teen Accused of Sexual Assaults in 2 Virginia High Schools." 4 NBC Washington, October 14, 2021, Teen Accused of Sexual Assaults in 2 Virginia Schools – NBC4 Washington (nbcwashington.com).

20. Standing for Freedom Center Staff, "Loudoun County School Board approves Virginia's transgender guidelines despite parents' opposition." Standing for Freedom Center, August 12, 2021, Loudoun County School Board approves Virginia's transgender guidelines despite parents' opposition – Standing for Freedom Center.

21. Virginia Aabram, "Teenager found guilty in Loudoun County bathroom assault." Washington Examiner, October 25, 2021, Updated October 26, 2021, Teenager found guilty in Loudoun County bathroom assault | Washington Examiner.

22. Standing for Freedom Center Staff, "Skirt-wearing male student is found guilty of raping a 15-year-old- girl in a school bathroom in Loudoun County, Virginia." Standing for Freedom Center, October 26, 2021, Skirt-wearing male student is found guilty of raping a 15-year-old girl in a school bathroom in Loudoun County, Virginia – Standing for Freedom Center.

23. Jennifer Smith and Shawn Cohen, "Family of schoolgirl raped in girls' bathroom asked judge to SPARE Loudoun County 'boy in a skirt,' 15, from jail to 'give him a fighting chance at becoming a better person': Judge grants probation despite blasting his 'scary' psych report." DailyMail.com, January 12, 2022, updated January 13, 2022, Loudoun County 'boy in a skirt' is spared prison after victim's family asked judge not to jail him | Daily Mail Online.

24. Brittany Bernstein, "Loudoun County Sheriff Says Superintendent Knew about Sexual Assault in Girls' Bathroom the Day It Happened." National Review, November 22, 2021, Loudoun County Sheriff Says Superintendent Knew about Sexual Assault in Girls' Bathroom The Day It Happened | National Review.

25. Tyler O'Neil and Lucas Y. Tomlinson, "Loudoun County teen at center of school sexual assault cases sentenced." Fox News, January 12, 2022, Loudoun County teen at center of school sexual assault cases sentenced | Fox News.

26. "A Pathway to Equitable Math Instruction." Homepage - Math Equity Toolkit (equitablemath.org).

27. "Dismantling Racism in Mathematics Instruction." A Pathway to Equitable Math Instruction, May 2021, 1_STRIDE1.pdf (equitablemath.org).

28. "Full NSBA Letter to Biden Administration and Department of Justice Memo." National School Boards Association, Letter Dated September 29, 2021, Parents Defending Education, November 29, 2021, Full NSBA Letter to Biden Administration and Department of Justice Memo - Parents Defending Education, Letter.pdf (defendinged.org).

29. Office of the Attorney, Washington, D.C. 20530, Department of Justice, October 4, 2021, Partnership Among Federal, State, Local, Tribal and Territorial Law Enforcement to Address Threats Against School Administrators, Board Members, Teachers, and Staff (justice.gov).

30. Liz George, "Report: Biden official requested school board association letter calling parents 'domestic terrorists.'" American Military News, January 11, 2022, Report: Biden official requested school board association letter calling parents 'domestic terrorists' | American Military News.

31. Caroline Downey, "Memo Confirms National School Board Group 'Actively Engaged' with White House While Drafting 'Domestic Terrorists' Letter." National Review, November 11, 2021, Memo Confirms National School Board Group 'Actively Engaged' with White House While Drafting 'Domestic Terrorists' Letter | National Review.

32. Tyler O'Neil, "NSBA coordinated with White House, DOJ before sending notorious 'domestic terrorists' letter: emails." Fox News, November 12, 2021, NSBA coordinated with White House, DOJ before sending notorious 'domestic terrorists' letter: emails | Fox News.

33. Timothy H.J. Nerozzi, "13 states sue Biden admin for any communications on FBI surveillance of parents protesting school boards." Fox News, March 4, 2022, 13 states sue Biden admin for any communications on FBI surveillance of parents protesting school boards | Fox News.

34. Adam Andrzejewski, "Panorama Education, Co-Founded By U.S. AG Merrick Garland's Son-In-Law, Contracted With 23,000 Public Schools and Raised

$76M From Investors." Forbes, October 12, 2021, Panorama Education, Co-Founded By U.S. AG Merrick Garland's Son-In-Law, Contracted With 23,000 Public Schools & Raised $76M From Investors (forbes.com).

35. Aaron Feuer, "Letter From Panorama Education's CEO: Our Stand Against Systemic Racism." Panorama Education, Letter From Panorama Education's CEO: Our Stand Against Systemic Racism.

36. "CS/CS/HB 1557: Parental Rights in Education." The Florida Senate, House Bill 1557 (2022) - The Florida Senate (flsenate.gov).

37. "CS/CS/HB 1557." Florida House of Representatives, _h1557er.docx (flsenate. gov).

38. "Governor Ron DeSantis Signs Historic Bill to Protect Parental Rights in Education." Ron DeSantis – 46th Governor of Florida, March 28, 2022, Governor Ron DeSantis Signs Historic Bill to Protect Parental Rights in Education (flgov.com).

39. "Statement by Press Secretary Karine Jean-Pierre on Florida's 'Don't Say Gay' Law Taking Effect." The White House, July 01, 2022, Statement by Press Secretary Karine Jean-Pierre on Florida's "Don't Say Gay" Law Taking Effect | The White House.

Chapter 8

1. Karl Marx and Frederick Engels, "Manifesto of the Communist Party." February 1848, Manifesto of the Communist Party (marxists.org).

2. S. Omarova, "The People's Ledger: How to Democratize Money and Finance the Economy." Semantic Scholar, Published October 20, 2020, [PDF] The People's Ledger: How to Democratize Money and Finance the Economy | Semantic Scholar.

3. "President Biden Announces Key Nominations for Financial Regulation and Investor Protection." The White House, September 23, 2021, President Biden Announces Key Nominations for Financial Regulation and Investor Protection | The White House.

4. "Toomey: I've Never Seen a Nominee with More Radical Ideas." United States Senate Committee on Banking, Housing and Urban Affairs, November 18, 2021, Toomey: I've Never Seen a Nominee with More Radical Ideas | United States Committee on Banking, Housing, and Urban Affairs (senate.gov).

5. Zachary Warmbrodt, "'Radical' Biden nominee faces backlash from banks." POLITICO, 9/24/2021, 'Radical' Biden nominee faces backlash from banks - POLITICO.

6. Hans Nichols, "Scoop: Centrist Dems sink Biden's nominee for top bank regulator." Axios, November 24, 2021, Scoop: Centrist Dems sink Biden's nominee for top bank regulator (axios.com).

7. "Statement of President Joe Biden and Nominee for Office of the Comptroller of the Currency Saule Omarova." The White House, December 07, 2021, Statement of President Joe Biden and Nominee for Office of the Comptroller of the Currency Saule Omarova | The White House.

8. Kyle Iboshi, "Feds quietly dismiss dozens of Portland protest cases." KGW8, March 2, 2021, Portland protests: Feds quietly dismiss dozens of cases | kgw. com.

9. "H.R. 5376 – Inflation Reduction Act of 2022." Congress.Gov, Actions - H.R.5376 - 117th Congress (2021-2022): Inflation Reduction Act of 2022 | Congress.gov | Library of Congress, Text - H.R.5376 - 117th Congress (2021-2022): Inflation Reduction Act of 2022 | Congress.gov | Library of Congress.

10. "BY THE NUMBERS: The Inflation Reduction Act." The White House, August 15, 2022, BY THE NUMBERS: The Inflation Reduction Act | The White House.

11. "Billionaires by Country 2022." World Population Review, Billionaires by Country 2022 (worldpopulationreview.com).

12. "The American Families Plan Tax Compliance Agenda." U.S. Department of the Treasury, May 2021, The-American-Families-Plan-Tax-Compliance-Agenda.pdf (treasury.gov).

13. "IRS Is Hiring New Employees, Not Raising an Army." Bloomberg Tax, Aug 18, 2022, IRS Is Hiring New Employees, Not Raising an Army (bloombergtax. com).

14. "Who monitors or oversees the FBI?" FBI, Who monitors or oversees the FBI? — FBI.

15. "The Court and Constitutional Interpretation." Supreme Court of the United States, The Court and Constitutional Interpretation - Supreme Court of the United States.

16. "History and Traditions." Supreme Court of the United States, History and Traditions (supremecourt.gov).

17. Barbara Sprunt, "Biden Says He's 'Not a Fan' Of Expanding The Supreme Court." NPR, October 13, 2020, Biden Says He's 'Not A Fan' Of Packing Supreme Court : NPR.

Chapter 9

1. "2020 election to cost $14 billion, blowing away spending records." Open Secrets, October 28, 2020, 2020 election to cost $14 billion, blowing away spending records • OpenSecrets.

2. Pennsylvania 2020 and 2016 Presidential Elections. Department of State, Pennsylvania Elections - County Breakdown Results (pa.gov).

3. "Report on the 2020 General Election." Pennsylvania Department of State, May 14, 2021, 2020-General-Election-Report.pdf (pa.gov).

4. "Election Results." Wisconsin Elections Commission, Election Results | Wisconsin Elections Commission.

5. Mili Godio, "Donald Trump Gained 4.4 Points in New York City in 2020, Compared With 2016." Newsweek, 12/4/20, Donald Trump Gained 4.4 Points in New York City in 2020, Compared With 2016 (newsweek.com).

6. "Prior Statewide Elections." California Secretary of State, November 3, 2020 and November 8, 2016, Prior Statewide Elections :: California Secretary of State.

7. "Election Results." Illinois State Board of Elections, Vote Total Search Election Results (il.gov).

8. Holly Otterbein, "Why Biden didn't do better in big cities." POLITICO, 11/15/2020, Why Biden didn't do better in big cities – POLITICO.

9. "Election Results – 1962 to Present." Official SOS ENR Website, Nevada Secretary of State, Election Results - 1962 to Present | Nevada Secretary of State (nvsos.gov).

10. Donald J. Trump, Official Facebook Page, Donald J. Trump | Facebook.

11. Jason Lange and Andy Sullivan, "House Republicans who challenged Biden's win are losing lots of corporate cash." Reuters, March 16, 2022, House Republicans who challenged Biden's win are losing lots of corporate cash | Reuters.

12. Barbara Sprunt, "Here Are the Republicans Who Objected To The Electoral College Count." NPR, January 7, 2021, Here Are The Republicans Who Objected To The Electoral College Count : Capitol Insurrection Updates : NPR.

13. Senators Kennedy, Dugan, et al., "Senate Bill 463 – A Bill To Be Entitled An Act." C:\pdf\191511.wpd (ga.gov).

14. Mark Niesse, "Bill to add Georgia precincts faces unexpected opponent: voting groups." The Atlanta Journal- Constitution, March 25, 2020, Voting rights groups oppose Georgia bill to fight long lines (ajc.com).

15. "GA SB463 – Actions." Bill Track, GA SB463 | BillTrack50.

16. "Georgia Senate Bill 202." LegiScan, GA SB202 | 2021-2022 | Regular Session | LegiScan, Bill Text: GA SB202 | 2021-2022 | Regular Session | Enrolled | LegiScan.

17. Andre M. Perry and Anthony Barr, "Georgia's voter suppression bill is an assault on our democracy." Brookings, April 19, 2021, Georgia's voter suppression bill is an assault on our democracy (brookings.edu).

18. Nick Corasaniti, "Georgia G.O.P. Passes Major Law to Limit Voting Amid Nationwide Push." The New York Times, March 25, 2021, Georgia G.O.P. Passes Major Law to Limit Voting - The New York Times (nytimes.com).

19. Kelly Mena, Fredreka Schouten, Dianne Gallagher, and Pamela Kirkland, "Georgia Republicans speed sweeping elections bill restricting voting access into law." CNN, Updated March 26, 2021, Georgia voting bill: Republicans speed sweeping elections bill restricting voting access into law | CNN Politics.

20. Michelle Stoddart, "Biden calls new GOP-passed Georgia law restricting voting access an 'atrocity.'" ABC News, March 26, 2021, Biden calls new GOP-passed Georgia law restricting voting access an 'atrocity' - ABC News.

21. "Statement by President Biden on the Attack on the Right to Vote in Georgia." The White House, March 26, 2021, Statement by President Biden on the Attack on the Right to Vote in Georgia | The White House.

22. Benjamin Din, "Biden endorses moving MLB All-Star Game out of Georgia." POLITICO, 3/31/2021, Biden endorses moving MLB All-Star Game out of Georgia - POLITICO.

23. Daniel Starkand, "Lakers News: Magic Johnson and LeBron James Praise MLB For Moving All-Star Game Out Of Atlanta." Lakers Nation, 4/4/2021, Lakers News: Magic Johnson & LeBron James Praise MLB For Moving All-Star Game Out Of Atlanta (lakersnation.com).

24. Michael Ruiz and Andrew Murray, "Dem-backed MLB All-Star Game move cost majority-Black Atlanta tens of millions of dollars." Fox Business, July 13, 2021, Dem-backed MLB All-Star Game move cost majority-Black Atlanta tens of millions of dollars | Fox Business.

25. WSBTV.com News Staff, "Georgia sees record early voting turnout during primary elections." WSB-TV2-Atlanta, May 22, 2022, Georgia sees record early voting turnout during primary elections – WSB-TV Channel 2 - Atlanta (wsbtv. com).

26. "Election List." Georgia Secretary of State, List Elections (clarityelections. com), Election Night Reporting (clarityelections.com), GA - Election Night Reporting (clarityelections.com), GA - Election Results (clarityelections.com).

27. "Georgia Election Law Results in Record Early-Voting Turnout." Georgia Secretary of State, May 21st, 2022, Georgia Election Law Results in Record Early-Voting Turnout | Georgia Secretary of State (ga.gov).

28. "Voter identification laws." Wikipedia, Voter identification laws - Wikipedia.

29. "Voting in a Federal Election." Elections Canada, September 2019, Voting in a Federal Election – Elections Canada.

30. "Electoral Registry." INE Instituto Nacional Electoral, April 22, 2017, Electoral Registry - Instituto Nacional Electoral (ine.mx).

31. Bernie Sanders, "Voter ID laws aren't really intended to discourage fraud." @ SenSanders, Twitter, Bernie Sanders on Twitter: "Voter ID laws aren't really intended to discourage fraud, they're intended to discourage voting. http://t.co/k6ZGDafzxC" / Twitter.

32. Bernie Sanders, "Free and Fair Elections." Bernie Sanders Official Website, Free and Fair Elections | Bernie Sanders Official Website.

33. "How to vote." The Election Authority, Att rösta (engelska).pdf (val.se).

34. "2022 Index of Economic Freedom." The Heritage Foundation, Country Rankings: World & Global Economy Rankings on Economic Freedom (heritage. org).

35. Nima Sanandaji, "Nordic Countries Aren't Actually Socialist." Foreign Policy. com, October 27, 2021, Nordic Countries Aren't Actually Socialist (foreign-policy.com).

Chapter 10

1. Richard Rosenfeld, "Overview and Reflections." Council on Criminal Justice, Overview and Reflections - Crime Bill (foleon.com).

2. "H.R. 3355 – Violent Crime Control and Law Enforcement Act of 1994." Congress.gov, H.R.3355 - 103rd Congress (1993-1994): Violent Crime Control and Law Enforcement Act of 1994 | Congress.gov | Library of Congress.

3. Statista Research Department, "Number of reported murder and nonnegligent manslaughter cases in the United States from 1990 to 2021." Statista, October 10, 2022, U.S.: reported murder and nonnegligent manslaughter cases 2021 | Statista.

4. Josiah Bates, "These Major Cities Reported the Highest Homicide Rates in 2021." TIME, October 19, 2022, These Cities Reported the Highest Homicide Rates in 2021 | Time.

5. Megan Sheets, "REVEALED: Top Chicago prosecutor Kim Foxx's office has dismissed more than 25,000 felony cases – including murders, shootings, sexual

assaults, and Jussie Smollett's 'hoax' attack." DailyMail.com, August 10, 2020, Updated March 10, 2022, Chicago prosecutor Kim Foxx dismissed over 25k felony cases | Daily Mail Online.

6. Rachel Hinton, "Another billionaire weighs in on state's attorney's race: George Soros gives $2M to group backing Foxx." CHICAGO SUN TIMES, February 20, 2020, George Soros gives $2 million to PAC backing Kim Foxx - Chicago Sun-Times (suntimes.com).

7. Mica Soellner, "Kim Foxx pledges to fix 'broken criminal justice system' in second term as Chicago prosecutor." Washington Examiner, December 7, 2020, Kim Foxx pledges to fix 'broken criminal justice system' in second term as Chicago prosecutor | Washington Examiner.

8. "Kim Foxx Cook County State's Attorney." Kim Foxx.Com, Kim Foxx For Cook County State's Attorney.

9. WGN Web Desk, Judy Wang, "55 shot, 11 killed across Chicago this weekend is city's deadliest in 2021." WGN9, May 24, 2021, 55 shot, 11 killed across Chicago this weekend is city's deadliest in 2021 | WGN-TV (wgntv.com).

10. "Annual Reports." Chicago Police Department, Annual Reports | Chicago Police Department.

11. Matt Rosenburg, "Five Reasons why the latest spin on Chicago's murder problem is dead wrong." Madison – St. Clair Record, Five reasons why the latest spin on Chicago's murder problem is dead wrong | Madison - St. Clair Record (madisonrecord.com).

12. Zach Smith and Charles Stimson, "Meet Kim Foxx, the Rogue Prosecutor Whose Policies are Wreaking Havoc in Chicago." The Heritage Foundation, Nov 3, 2020, Meet Kim Foxx, the Rogue Prosecutor Whose Policies are Wreaking Havoc in Chicago | The Heritage Foundation.

13. "Bill Status of HB3653." Illinois General Assembly, Illinois General Assembly - Bill Status for HB3653 (ilga.gov).

14. "HB 3653: What's Included in the Bill Being Signed Into Law Monday." NBC 5 Chicago, February 22, 2021, HB 3653: What's Included in the Bill Being Signed Into Law Monday – NBC Chicago.

15. "Summary of Provisions in Illinois House Bill 3653: Criminal Justice Omnibus Bill." The Civic Federation, February 15, 2021, Summary of Provisions in Illinois House Bill 3653: Criminal Justice Omnibus Bill | The Civic Federation.

16. "Illinois Police Reform Bill 2021: The start of a dangerous trend for police?" National Police Support Fund, March 25, 2021, Illinois Police Reform Bill 2021: The start of a dangerous trend for police? - National Police Support Fund.

17. Marsha Heller, "Gov. Pritzker signs controversial justice reform bill." KFVS12, Updated February 22, 2021, Gov. Pritzker signs controversial justice reform bill (kfvs12.com).

18. Matt Masterson, "Pritzker Signs Sweeping Criminal Justice Reform Bill Into Law." WTTW, February 22, 2021, Pritzker Signs Sweeping Criminal Justice Reform Bill Into Law | Chicago News | WTTW.

19. Patrick Andriesen, "Illinois' 2nd-highest gas taxes drive motorists, business across state lines." Illinois Policy, April 19, 2022, Illinois' 2nd-highest gas taxes drive motorists, business across state lines (illinoispolicy.org).

20. Derek Cantu, NPR Illinois, "Private School Advocates Urge Pritzker To Leave Scholarship Donation Tax Credits Alone." ILLINOIS NEWSROOM, May 26, 2021, Private School Advocates Urge Pritzker To Leave Scholarship Donation Tax Credits Alone - Illinois Newsroom.

21. "Comparison of Other States' General Obligation Bond Ratings." California State Treasurer, PFD Current Credit Ratings (ca.gov).

22. "Cook County Medical Examiner's Office Registers Record Number of Gun-Related Homicides in 2021." Cook County Government, 01/03/2022, Cook County Medical Examiner's Office Registers Record Number of Gun-Related Homicides in 2021 (cookcountyil.gov).

23. Craig Wall, "Gov. Pritzker joins conference of governors, mayors meeting with Biden about infrastructure plan." ABC7 Chicago, July 14, 2021, Governor JB Pritzker joins conference of governors, mayors meeting with President Joe Biden about infrastructure plan - ABC7 Chicago.

24. Jessica D'Onofrio, Evelyn Holmes, Liz Nagy and ABC Chicago Digital Team, "2 teens charged after Vietnam vet dies in Hyde Park carjacking attempt: police." ABC7 Chicago, July 16, 2021, Hyde Park carjacking: 2 charged after man, 73, dies in beating near University of Chicago - ABC7 Chicago.

25. "17-Year-Old Denied Bond in Fatal Attempted Carjacking of Vietnam Veteran Keith Cooper." CBS Chicago, July 17, 2021, 17-Year-Old Denied Bond In Fatal Attempted Carjacking Of Vietnam Veteran Keith Cooper - CBS Chicago (cbsnews.com).

26. Lynn Sweet, "Kamala Harris heads to Chicago Tuesday to focus on vaccine equity." Chicago Sun-Times, March 31, 2021, Vice President Kamala Harris travels to Chicago on Tuesday: Visit to focus on COVID vaccine equity - Chicago Sun-Times (suntimes.com).

27. Mitchell Armentrout, "VP Kamala Harris urges Chicagoans to get vaccinated and stay safe: 'In that way we will build back up.'" Chicago Sun-Times, April 6, 2021, Vice President Kamala Harris visits Chicago and urges residents to get the coronavirus vaccine - Chicago Sun-Times (suntimes.com).

28. "Remarks by Vice President Harris at the Generation Equality Forum." The White House, June 30, 2021, Remarks by Vice President Harris at the Generation Equality Forum | The White House.

29. Gabrielle Fonrouge, "This is why Jacob Blake had a warrant out for his arrest." New York Post, August 28, 2020, This is why Jacob Blake had a warrant out for his arrest (nypost.com).

30. Jason Silverstein, "Kamala Harris meets with Jacob Blake's family in Wisconsin." CBS News, September 8, 2020, Kamala Harris meets with Jacob Blake's family in Wisconsin - CBS News.

31. Jill Martin, Leah Asmelash and David Close, "These teams and athletes refused to play in protest of the Jacob Blake shooting." CNN, August 28, 2020, These teams and athletes refused to play in protest of the Jacob Blake shooting | CNN.

32. "NBA Finals Ratings History (1988-Present)." Sports Media Watch, NBA Finals Ratings History (1988-Present) - Sports Media Watch.

33. Dan Wetzel, "LiAngelo Ball and UCLA teammates could face 3-10 years in prison if convicted of shoplifting." Yahoo, November 7, 2017, LiAngelo Ball facing 3-10 years in prison if convicted (yahoo.com).

34. Kyle Boone, "Donald Trump asked China's president to help LiAngelo Ball, 2 other UCLA players." CBSSPORTS.com, November 13, 2017, Donald Trump asked China's president to help LiAngelo Ball, 2 other UCLA players - CBSSports.com.

35. Isabel Gonzalez, "Russia confirms it seeks convicted arms dealer in potential prisoner swap for WNBA star Brittney Griner." CBSSPORTS.com, August 13, 2022, Russia confirms it seeks convicted arms dealer in potential prisoner swap for WNBA star Brittney Griner - CBSSports.com.

36. Dave McMenamin, "LeBron James says Black Community 'terrified' of police conduct." ESPN, August 25, 2020, LeBron James says Black community 'terrified' of police conduct (espn.com).

37. "Report on the Officer Involved Shooting of Jacob Blake." County of Kenosha, Microsoft Word - Draft 7.0.docx (kenoshacounty.org).

38. David K. Li and Diana Dasrath, "Sexual assault charge against Jacob Blake dismissed in plea agreement." NBC News, November 6, 2020, Sexual assault charge against Jacob Blake dismissed in plea agreement (nbcnews.com).

39. Doha Madani, "Kenosha officer who shot Jacob Blake won't face discipline, police chief says." NBC News, April 13, 2021, Kenosha officer who shot Jacob Blake won't face discipline, police chief says (nbcnews.com).

40. "Law Enforcement Officers Shot And Killed In The Line Of Duty." National Fraternal Order of Police, 3 January 2022, report-20220103-shot-killed-monthly-report.pdf (fop.net).

41. Sean Emery and Eric Licas, Orange County Register, "2 L.A. County Sheriff's deputies shot in Compton ambush caught on surveillance video; both in critical condition." Press-Telegram, September 12, 2020, Updated September 13, 2020, 2 L.A. County Sheriff's deputies shot in Compton ambush caught on surveillance video; both in critical condition – Press Telegram.

42. "Convicted Felon Deonte Murray Charged In Compton Ambush Shooting of 2 LA Deputies." CBS Los Angeles, September 30, 2020, Convicted Felon Deonte Murray Charged In Compton Ambush Shooting Of 2 LA Deputies - CBS Los Angeles (cbsnews.com).

43. "Two Brothers, Monte And Eric Morgan, Charged In Fatal Shooting of Chicago Police Officer Ella French." CBS Chicago, August 10, 2021, Two Brothers, Monte And Eric Morgan, Charged In Fatal Shooting Of Chicago Police Officer Ella French - CBS Chicago (cbsnews.com).

44. Jessica D'Onofrio, Liz Nagy, and Alexis McAdams, "Surveillance video shows traffic stop before fatal shooting of CPD Officer Ella French, 2 charged." ABC7 Chicago, August 10, 2021, Chicago police shooting: Surveillance video shows traffic stop before Chicago Police Officer Ella French killed, 2 charged - ABC7 Chicago.

45. "Alleged buyer of gun used in officer Ella French's murder defends himself but Chicago's police chief is outraged that he's out on bond." CBS News, August 12, 2021, Alleged buyer of gun used in officer Ella French's murder defends himself but Chicago's police chief is outraged that he's out on bond - CBS News.

46. Mike Lowe, "Fallen officer Ella French helped save life of infant wounded in Englewood mass shooting." WGN9, August 10, 2021, Fallen officer Ella French helped save life of infant wounded in Englewood mass shooting | WGN-TV (wgntv.com).

47. Matt Rosenburg, "It's open season on Chicago police: Shootings at cops up fourfold in 2020, 2021." Madison St. Clair Record, June, 8, 2022, It's open season on Chicago police: Shootings at cops up fourfold in 2020, 2021 | Madison - St. Clair Record (madisonrecord.com).

48. Nick Selbe, "LeBron James Addresses Deleted Tweet on Police Shooting of Ma'Khia Bryant." SI, April 22, 2021, LeBron posts, explains deleted tweet on Columbus police shooting - Sports Illustrated.

49. "Ohio officer cleared in fatal shooting of teenager Ma'Khia Bryant." CBS News, March 11, 2022, Ohio officer cleared in fatal shooting of teenager Ma'Khia Bryant - CBS News.

50. Camille Caldera, "Fact check: Rates of White-on-White and Black-on-Black crime are similar." USA Today, September 29, 2020, Fact check: Meme shows incorrect homicide stats by race (usatoday.com).

51. Priya Krishnakumar and Peter Nickeas, "10 of the country's most populous cities set homicide records last year." CNN, January 4, 2022, US homicides: 10 of the country's most populous cities set records last year | CNN.

52. "Crime Maps and Stats." Philadelphia Police Department, Crime Maps & Stats | Philadelphia Police Department (phillypolice.com).

53. Mike D'Onofrio, "Philadelphia homicides hit historic level in 2021." AXIOS Philadelphia, January 10, 2022, Philadelphia homicides hit historic level in 2021 - Axios Philadelphia.

54. Mark Lungariello, "Philadelphia cops ID pregnant woman shot to death as city homicides approach record." New York Post, November 24, 2021, Pregnant Philadelphia woman shot Jessica Covington ID'ed as homicides approach record (nypost.com).

55. "Shooting Incident Statistics." The City of Portland, Oregon – Police Bureau, Shooting Incident Statistics | The City of Portland, Oregon (portlandoregon. gov).

56. "Portland Homicide Problem Analysis 2019-2021." Portland Police Bureau, California Partnership for Safe Communities, PowerPoint Presentation (port-land.gov).

57. Bay City News, "Police Crime Data for 2021 Show Homicides, Gun Violence Saw Significant Increases." NBC Bay Area, January 26, 2022, Police Crime Data for 2021 Show Homicides, Gun Violence Saw Significant Increases – NBC Bay Area.

58. Matt Boone, "Family of Asian grandmother stabbed at San Francisco bus stop in 'shock and disbelief.'" ABC 7 News, May 5, 2021, San Francisco stabbing: Family of 85-year-old Asian grandmother stabbed at bus stop in 'shock and disbelief' - ABC7 San Francisco (abc7news.com).

59. Michael Barba, "Suspect in Market Street stabbings told police he had no regrets, DA says." San Francisco Examiner, May 13, 2021, Suspect in Market Street stabbings told police he had no regrets, DA says | Archives | sfexaminer. com.

60. Dion Lim, "Exclusive: Former security guard recalls brutal 2017 attack by SF stabbing suspect." ABC 7 News, May 7, 2021, EXCLUSIVE: Former security guard recalls brutal 2017 attack by Patrick Thompson - ABC7 San Francisco (abc7news.com).

61. "Chesa Boudin recall, San Francisco, California (2021-2022)." Ballotpedia, Chesa Boudin recall, San Francisco, California (2021-2022) - Ballotpedia.

62. "H.R. 1280 - George Floyd Justice in Policing Act of 2021." Congress.Gov, H.R.1280 - 117th Congress (2021-2022): George Floyd Justice in Policing Act of 2021 | Congress.gov | Library of Congress.

63. "Statement of Administration Policy, H.R. 1280 – George Floyd Justice in Policing Act of 2021." Executive Office of the President, SAP H.R. 1280 (whitehouse.gov).

64. "Pass the George Floyd Justice in Policing Act (HR 1280)." National Education Association, Submitted on March 1, 2021, Pass the George Floyd Justice in Policing Act (HR 1280) | NEA.

65. Mike Gonzalez, "What the Media Doesn't Want You To Know About 2020's Record Murder Spike." The Heritage Foundation, Oct 7, 2021, What the Media Doesn't Want You To Know About 2020's Record Murder Spike | The Heritage Foundation.

66. Curtis Bunn, "Report: Black people are still killed by police at a higher rate than other groups." NBC News, March 3, 2022, Report: Black people are still killed by police at a higher rate than other groups (nbcnews.com)

67. Ryan Young and Devon M Sayers, "Why police forces are struggling to recruit and keep officers." CNN, February 3, 2022, Why police forces are struggling to recruit and keep officers | CNN.

68. "Burnout And Low Turnout Of Applicants Leaving CPD With Officer Shortage; 'People Don't Want To Be The Police.'" CBS Chicago, October 11, 2021, Burnout And Low Turnout Of Applicants Leaving CPD With Officer Shortage; 'People Don't Want To Be The Police' - CBS Chicago (cbsnews.com).

69. Shane Dixon Kavanaugh, "Why Portland has fewer cops now than any point in past 30 years." Police1, November 08, 2021, Why Portland has fewer cops now than any point in past 30 years (police1.com).

70. Stephanie Sierra, "San Francisco police chief explains what's driving dire staffing issues; nearly 600 officers short." ABC 7 News, April 14, 2022, San Francisco Police Dept. grapples with losing 100 officers a year amid worst staffing shortage - ABC7 San Francisco (abc7news.com).

71. Missouri State Highway Patrol, Beyond 20/20 Perspective - View report (mo.gov).

72. Kansas City, Missouri, Police Department, "Daily Homicide Analysis." Daily Homicide Analysis - HOM001 (kcpd.org).

73. "2023 Homicide Analysis." Saint Louis Police Department, HIT0001 (slmpd.org).

74. Jack Grone, "Violent Crime In Saint Louis County Fell in 2021, But Remains Elevated Overall." McPherson Publishing, July 29, 2022, Violent Crime In

St. Louis County Fell In 2021, But Remains Elevated Overall | McPherson (mcphersonpublishing.com).

75. Samuel Stebbins, "How the Murder Rate in Missouri Compares to the Rest of the Country." 24/7 Wall St., December 10, 2021, How the Murder Rate in Missouri Compares to the Rest of the Country - 24/7 Wall St. (247wallst.com).

76. "Violent Crime 2020." Tennessee Crime Stats, Violent Crime 2020 (tn.gov).

77. Destinee Hannah, "Memphis breaks homicide record for 2nd year in a row." WREG Memphis, January 3, 2022, Memphis breaks homicide record for 2nd year in a row (wreg.com).

78. "Crime in Illinois 2020 – Annual Uniform Crime Report." Illinois State Police, CII 2020 Final w Covers.pdf (illinois.gov).

79. Alix Martichoux and Cornell Barnard, "San Francisco Mayor London Breed announces cuts to police in new city budget." ABC 7 News, July 31, 2020, San Francisco to cut funding to police, sheriff's departments in new budget, Mayor London Breed announces - ABC7 San Francisco (abc7news.com).

80. Barnini Chakraborty, "Democratic mayors who called to defund the police spent millions on own security details." Washington Examiner, July 21, 2021, Democratic mayors who called to defund the police spent millions on own security details | Washington Examiner.

81. "Guns in the U.S.- 2021 Second-Highest Year for Gun Sales Since 2000." SafeHome.org, Guns in the U.S. – 2021 Second-Highest Year for Gun Sales Since 2000 (safehome.org).

82. David Maccar, "Gun Sales 2021: 5.4 Million Americans Bought A Firearm For The First Time." Free Range American, January 26, 2022, Gun Sales 2021: 5.4 Million Americans Bought a Firearm for the First Time (freerangeamerican.us).

83. David Kopel and Vincent Harinam, "In the wake of a gun ban, Venezuela sees rising homicide rate." The Hill, 4/19/18, In the wake of a gun ban, Venezuela sees rising homicide rate | The Hill.

84. "Venezuela bans private gun ownership." BBC News, June 1, 2012, Venezuela bans private gun ownership - BBC News.

85. Indrees Ali, Patricia Zengerle and Jonathan Landay, "Planes, guns, night-vision goggles: The Taliban's new U.S.-made war chest." Reuters, August 19, 2021, Planes, guns, night-vision goggles: The Taliban's new U.S.-made war chest | Reuters.

86. Jared Keller, "Here's all the US military equipment that likely ended up in Taliban hands." TASK & PURPOSE, August 18, 2021, Here's all the US military equipment that likely ended up in Taliban hands (taskandpurpose.com).

87. Adam Andrzejewski, "Biden Administration Erased Afghan Weapons Reports From Federal Websites." Forbes, August 31, 2021, Biden Administration Erased Afghan Weapons Reports From Federal Websites (forbes.com).

88. "List of U.S. states and territories by intentional homicide rate." Wikipedia, List of U.S. states and territories by intentional homicide rate - Wikipedia.

89. "Underlying Cause of Death – All Ages." Illinois Department of Public Health, Website data - Deaths 2020.xlsx (illinois.gov)

Chapter 11

1. Bryce Hill, "79% OF Illinois Communities Lose People In 2021; Chicago Loses 45K." Illinois Policy, May 25, 2022, 79% of Illinois communities lose people in 2021; Chicago loses 45K (illinoispolicy.org).

2. "Election List." Georgia Secretary of State, List Elections (clarityelections.com).

3. "1992 – Current Election History." Office of the Secretary of State, HISTORICAL ELECTIONS - OFFICIAL RESULTS (state.tx.us).

4. "Texas Election Results." Texas Secretary of State, ::Texas Election Night Results:: (texas-election.com).

5. "Key Reasons Why Millions Are Moving to Texas." AP, May 21, 2021, Key Reasons Why Millions Are Moving to Texas | AP News.

6. Anshool Deshmukh, "Mapped: Visualizing U.S. Oil Production by State." Visual Capitalist, August 10, 2021, Mapped: U.S. Oil Production by State - Visual Capitalist.

7. "List of United States cities by population." Wikipedia, List of United States cities by population - Wikipedia.

8. Alexa Mae Asperin, "70% of San Francisco residents say quality of life has declined: poll." KRON4, June 22, 2021, 70% of San Francisco residents say quality of life has declined: poll | KRON4.

9. Eric Ting, "Don't look now but San Francisco's poop problem seems to be getting better." SFGATE, July 13, 2021, Don't look now but San Francisco's poop problem seems to be getting better (sfgate.com).

10. "Where people in California are moving to most." Stacker, July 6, 2022, Where People in California Are Moving to Most | Stacker.

11. "What is causing Californians to leave California?" The Sun, March 23, 2022, What is causing Californians to leave California? – San Bernardino Sun (sbsun.com).

12. Dymond Green, "The California exodus continues as residents head south of the border." CNBC, June 11, 2022, Updated June 13, 2022, Californians working from home are moving to Mexico amid inflation (cnbc.com).

13. Eli Yokley, "Biden's Net Approval Rating Is Underwater in 40 States." Morning Consult, April 26, 2022, Biden Approval Rating is Down in 40 States (morning-consult.com).

14. "List of U.S. states and territories by median age." Wikipedia, List of U.S. states and territories by median age - Wikipedia.

15. "What Redistricting Looks Like In Every State." FiveThirtyEight, What Redistricting Looks Like In Every State - Florida | FiveThirtyEight. What Redistricting Looks Like In Every State - Illinois | FiveThirtyEight.

www.ingramcontent.com/pod-product-compliance
Lightning Source LLC
Chambersburg PA
CBHW062217270326
41930CB00009B/1765